Social Issues in
IMF-Supported Programs

Sanjeev Gupta, Louis Dicks-Mireaux, Ritha Khemani,
Calvin McDonald, and Marijn Verhoeven

INTERNATIONAL MONETARY FUND
Washington DC
2000

Production: IMF Graphics Section
Typesetting: Jack Federici
Figures: In-Ok Yoon

Cataloging-in-Publication Data

Social issues in IMF-supported programs / Sanjeev Gupta . . .
    [et al.]. – Washington, D.C. : International Monetary Fund, 2000.
        p.   cm. — (Occasional paper, 0251-6365 ; no. 191)
    Includes bibliographical references.
    ISBN 1-55775-873-5
    1. International Monetary Fund.   2. Social policy.   3. Expenditures,
Public.   I. Gupta, Sanjeev.   II. International Monetary Fund.
III. Occasional Paper (International Monetary Fund) ; no. 191.

HG3881.5.I58S664 2000

Price: US$18.00
(US$15.00 to full-time faculty members and
students at universities and colleges)

Please send orders to:
International Monetary Fund, Publication Services
700 19th Street, N.W., Washington, D.C. 20431, U.S.A.
Tel.: (202) 623-7430   Telefax: (202) 623-7201
E-mail: publications@imf.org
Internet: http://www.imf.org

recycled paper

Contents

Boxes

Tables

Figures

The following symbols have been used throughout this paper:

. . . to indicate that data are not available;

—   to indicate that the figure is zero or less than half the final digit shown, or that the item
       does not exist;

–   between years or months (e.g., 1994–95 or January–June) to indicate the years or
       months covered, including the beginning and ending years or months;

/   between years (e.g., 1994/95) to indicate a crop or fiscal (financial) year.

"Billion" means a thousand million.

Minor discrepancies between constituent figures and totals are due to rounding.

The term "country," as used in this paper, does not in all cases refer to a territorial entity that
is a state as understood by international law and practice; the term also covers some territorial
entities that are not states, but for which statistical data are maintained and provided internationally on a separate and independent basis.

Preface

As part of its mandate, the IMF seeks to create the conditions necessary for sustained high-quality growth, which encompasses a broad range of elements. These include sound macroeconomic policies, growth-enhancing structural reforms, good governance, and social policies such as cost-effective social safety nets and targeted social expenditures. Over the years, the IMF and the international community have increasingly recognized that macroeconomic and structural policies have important social implications, which in turn have ramifications for the domestic ownership of economic and reform agendas and promoting sustainable growth. In particular, social safety nets aimed at cushioning the adverse social impact of adjustment programs on vulnerable groups have become increasingly important. Also, there has been greater focus on the prioritization of public spending on areas of social policies that promote growth through poverty reduction, specifically with regard to increased access of the poor to education, health, and economic opportunity. The IMF has, therefore, taken a progressively more active stance on social policies to ensure that they are well integrated into IMF-supported programs and IMF policy advice. A key element of the IMF's involvement in social policies has been collaboration with other relevant international agencies, especially the World Bank, in order to draw upon their social policy expertise.

This paper—the most recent of a series of reviews of the IMF's involvement in social issues undertaken since the late 1970s—reviews the IMF's policy advice in two key areas of social policy: social safety nets and public spending on education and health care. It was initiated as part of the work by the World Bank and IMF to strengthen the poverty focus of adjustment programs in low-income countries, in particular within the framework of the Initiative for Heavily Indebted Poor Countries (HIPCs). This review looks at such social policies in IMF-supported programs in two broad groups of countries. The first group comprises a sample of up to 65 countries that implemented IMF-supported programs between 1985 and 1997. The second group comprises a sample of up to 12 countries that implemented programs under the IMF's Enhanced Structural Adjustment Facility (ESAF), including under the HIPC Initiative, during the latter part of the 1990s. The paper pulls together the main lessons from this experience and sets out proposals for strengthening the social content of IMF-supported programs including through mechanisms to strengthen World Bank–IMF collaboration in the social policy area. An earlier version of the paper was discussed by the IMF Executive Board on September 13, 1999; a summary by the Chairman of this Board discussion appears following the review.

Soon after these and other discussions (at the IMF and World Bank) on how to strengthen the poverty focus of adjustment programs in low-income countries, it was agreed at the IMF–World Bank 1999 Annual Meetings to put poverty reduction at the center of adjustment programs supported by the international community in the poorest countries. To implement this significant shift in policies, poverty reduction was made one of the central objectives of the ESAF, which was renamed the Poverty Reduction and Growth Facility (PRGF) on November 22, 1999; this will also be a key element of the enhanced initiative for debt reduction. A central feature of the PRGF is the Poverty Reduction Strategy Paper (PRSP)—one of the policy recommendations of this review—which articulates a country's comprehensive strategy for poverty reduction and integrates macroeconomic, structural, and social policies. The PRSP will be nationally owned and prepared through a broad participatory approach.

A number of IMF staff guided and contributed to this paper. In particular, the authors would like to thank Jack Boorman, Vito Tanzi, Peter Heller, Thomas Leddy, Ke-young Chu, and Russell Kincaid for substantial comments on earlier drafts; Hamid Davoodi, Frank Engels, Tetsuya Konuki, Henry Ma,

and Gustavo Yamada for contributions to various sections of the paper; and Randa Sab and Erwin Tiongson for providing statistical assistance. The authors are also grateful to staff of departments within the IMF and the World Bank for feedback on the earlier versions. Cecilia Pineda, Larry Hartwig, and Cecilia Lon performed the administrative tasks related to the production of the paper and Jeanette Morrison of the IMF's External Relations Department edited the Occasional Paper and coordinated its production.

Overview

This paper reviews the IMF's policy advice in two key areas of social policy: *social safety nets* and *public spending on education and health care.* While the IMF has been helping countries promote sustainable economic growth, and thereby reduce poverty through macroeconomic policy advice, it has also been strengthening its dialogue with member countries on the social implications of its advice. This paper offers preliminary conclusions on how to improve the integration of IMF policy advice on social safety nets and public social spending into program design[1] within a sustainable macroeconomic framework.

In the family of international organizations, the social components of country programs are primarily the responsibility of the World Bank and other organizations, not the IMF. The World Bank has primary mandates, responsibilities, and expertise on social issues. Whenever feasible, the IMF has drawn, and will continue to draw, upon the work of the World Bank and other organizations. Hence, enhanced inputs from and closer collaboration with these organizations are essential. Another important element is more dialogue with civil society groups, in particular labor unions and nongovernmental organizations (NGOs).

Social Safety Nets

The design of social safety nets and the timing of their establishment in countries have been influenced by both social protection needs and constraints. The needs reflected the specific adverse social effects of reform measures and the characteristics of affected groups. The constraints reflected the availability of social policy instruments such as old age pensions and unemployment insurance, and administrative and financing capacity. Whenever so-

cial policy instruments were available, the foremost challenges have been to ensure their targeting and to increase their financing.

This review identifies three key requirements for strengthening social safety nets in IMF-supported programs:

- more comprehensive ex ante analysis of the likely social impact of key macroeconomic and structural reform measures; such analysis needs to be undertaken before or at the time of program formulation;
- adequate follow-up of performance and monitoring of safety nets during program implementation to ensure that intended poor groups receive sufficient support; and
- introducing appropriate social policy instruments before the onset of crises and economic reforms.

IMF staff needs to rely on the expertise of the World Bank and other organizations in conducting the ex ante analysis. IMF staff reports should discuss such analysis and also the performance of social safety nets. When the World Bank or other relevant international institutions are unable to provide needed advice within a suitable time frame, IMF staff should attempt to fill the gap. These situations, however, should be infrequent.

Public Spending on Education and Health Care

On average, in the past decade, education and health care spending has increased—in real per capita terms, as well as in relation to GDP—in countries with IMF-supported programs. For many countries, these increases have been accompanied by improvements in a broad range of social indicators. Still, countries differ considerably on spending relative to GDP for both education and health care and on the speed of improvement of social indicators, reflecting in part differences in the efficiency of public spending.

There is scope for improving the efficiency and targeting of *existing* spending on education and

---

[1]For program descriptions see the Glossary at the end of this volume. After this paper was drafted, the Enhanced Stuctural Adjustment Facility (ESAF) was renamed the Poverty Reduction and Growth Facility (PRGF).

health care as a means of improving social indicators. This improvement could be achieved through, among other things, strengthening budget formulation and implementation capacity, increasing resources spent on primary education and basic health care, and reducing excessive out-of-pocket expenses borne by the poor in the form of user charges for primary education and basic health care. To consolidate the progress already made, this review identifies some steps that should be taken in programs supported by the IMF for

- establishing quantitative targets for education and health care spending more systematically, particularly for primary education and for basic health care; these targets should be reported in IMF staff papers for the Executive Board, and efforts should be made to strengthen the monitoring of such spending;
- occasionally setting performance criteria on minimum spending thresholds; and
- in some circumstances, monitoring budgetary allocations for selected key inputs, such as books and medicine (although an excessive level of detail in IMF-supported programs would be neither feasible nor appropriate).

These steps should be taken, in collaboration with the World Bank, by building on the progress that has already been achieved. IMF staff should continue to assess budgetary allocations for social sectors, relying on available World Bank input, in particular on timely Public Expenditure Reviews (PERs). To help promote social reform, IMF-supported programs could use as reference points the targets established by the authorities for selected *intermediate* social indicators (e.g., primary and secondary school enrollment rates and immunization rates). Especially where social indicators are failing to improve, despite increases in public spending, IMF staff should report to the Executive Board on discussions with the country authorities, World Bank, NGOs, and other institutions.

World Bank–IMF Collaboration

World Bank–IMF collaboration could be significantly improved by better integrating macroeconomic and social objectives, policy measures, and related work agendas. A shared understanding of the key social and macroeconomic issues is essential.

- Such collaboration could take place through the formulation of a poverty reduction strategy together with the country authorities in a participatory process. The main elements of the strategy would be set forth in a Poverty Reduction Strategy Paper (PRSP), which would be endorsed by the government, the World Bank, and the IMF. The PRSP would set out medium-term macro-economic, structural, and social policies consistent with the government's poverty reduction objectives. An IMF- or Bank-supported program should be consistent with the policy framework contained in the country-strategy paper.
- When timely World Bank input is either not available or insufficient, program design should allow for the fuller integration of relevant social policies at a later stage (e.g., at the time of program reviews), as additional analysis becomes available.

The PRSP should include several components that would facilitate World Bank–IMF collaboration. These components, which would reflect the two institutions' respective operational responsibilities in a country, should contain policy advice, financing needs, and work programs, in particular in the context of IMF-supported programs and World Bank lending operations.[2] Through this process, an iterative dialogue between the staffs of the IMF and the World Bank would be intensified, assuring the consistency between a macroeconomic framework and a cost-effective strategy for sustainable growth with poverty reduction.

The social policy components of the countries' Comprehensive Development Frameworks (CDFs) could also be integrated into their macroeconomic programs. In this regard, drawing upon the advice of the World Bank, the authorities should formulate, at an *early* stage of their macroeconomic programs, comprehensive social strategies that include specific action plans that provide a much-needed road map from objectives to policies. High-level poverty monitoring units in governments could help strengthen coordination at the local, national, and international levels and collect data for monitoring social progress.

Data and Institutional Capacity

IMF staff should make an effort to identify and highlight data weaknesses in the area of social spending indicators and social protection arrangements. This would help draw the authorities' attention to the urgent need to redress the data weaknesses in collaboration with the World Bank and other international agencies. In this regard, IMF staff should also assess the scope for technical assistance. Greater attention could also be given to inputs prepared by civic groups, NGOs, and donors.

---

[2]A more detailed discussion of the proposed Poverty Reduction Strategy Paper is provided in the World Bank–IMF staff paper, "HIPC Initiative—Strengthening the Link Between Debt Relief and Poverty Reduction," which is available on the Internet: http://www.imf.org/external/np/pdr/prsp/status.htm. See also the Glossary at the end of this volume.

I   Introduction

The IMF's mandate is, among other things, "to facilitate the expansion and balanced growth of international trade, and to contribute thereby to the promotion and maintenance of high levels of employment and real income . . . of all members as primary objectives of economic policy."[3] To this end, the IMF promotes sound macroeconomic policies, growth-enhancing structural reforms, and good social policies—conditions for high-quality growth. The IMF has paid increasing attention to these considerations in its policy advice.

This paper explores how attention to social issues can be accentuated. It is one of several papers that respond to the request of G-7/G-8 Finance Ministers at the June 1999 Cologne Summit to the World Bank and IMF to work together to strengthen social policies in the design of adjustment programs to protect the most vulnerable and to develop an enhanced framework for poverty reduction.[4] It looks at two social policy issues that are important for economic reform and growth—social safety nets and public social sector spending. It also identifies ways to better integrate sound social policies into the IMF's policy advice and program design within a sustainable macroeconomic framework.[5]

This paper examines the experiences of two sets of sample country groups. The first set comprises large samples of up to 65 countries with programs supported by the IMF, including the countries that implemented Stand-By Arrangements and programs supported by the Enhanced Structural Adjustment Facility (ESAF) from 1985 to 1997; the analysis aims to identify broad patterns and reach general conclusions. The second set comprises samples of 11–12 countries that implemented ESAF programs, including under the Initiative for Heavily Indebted Poor Countries (HIPCs), during the latter half of the 1990s; the analysis focuses on the use and monitoring of program targets. (See the Glossary for descriptions of these facilities.) The availability of data influenced the choice of countries, which may introduce some bias.

To a large extent, the analysis and policy advice on social issues lie outside the areas of IMF expertise. IMF staff relies on inputs from other international agencies, notably the World Bank. Thus, this paper also discusses collaboration with the World Bank and other agencies in the social policy sphere, including on internationally accepted principles, goals, practices, and indicators, such as those developed collaboratively by the Organization for Economic Cooperation and Development (OECD), United Nations (UN), and World Bank.

The paper has six sections. Section II describes the evolution of the IMF's social policy advice. Issues related to social safety nets as a mechanism to mitigate the immediate adverse effects of economic crises and reform programs on poor groups are presented in Section III. In Section IV we set out policy issues concerning the adequate provision of education and health care services—crucial for achieving countries' social development goals. We discuss IMF collaboration with the World Bank and other international organizations in Section V. Section VI, an afterword, briefly describes the IMF's new Poverty Reduction and Growth Facility, which replaced the Enhanced Structural Growth Facility in November 1999.

---

[3]Article I (ii) of the Articles of Agreement of the International Monetary Fund.

[4]See also the World Bank paper, "Building Poverty Reduction Strategies in Developing Countries" and the joint World Bank–IMF paper, "HIPC Initiative—Strengthening the Link Between Debt Relief and Poverty Reduction." Both are available on the Internet: http://www.imf.org/external/np/pdr/prsp/status.htm.

[5]The scope of social policies, and the channels through which macroeconomic policies can have a social impact, cover a broad area. The selective focus of this paper on social safety nets and public spending on education and health care allows in-depth consideration of a limited number of important social policies that are closely linked to the design of economic programs. For this reason, the focus is on the expenditure side of the budget, which has offered better opportunities than the tax side for poverty reduction (see Harberger, 1998). Likewise, the paper does not discuss the social impact of the IMF's macroeconomic policy advice, per se, except to the extent it bears directly on the design of social policies; nor does it attempt a broader review of IMF policy recommendations in the social sphere in bilateral and multilateral surveillance.

II Evolution of the IMF's Social Policy Advice

Sound economic policies favor both growth and the poor. The contribution of macroeconomic and structural reforms to long-run economic growth and poverty reduction is now well established. Research has demonstrated that low fiscal deficits and price stability promote economic growth,[6] and economic growth is the most significant single element that contributes to poverty reduction.[7] Macroeconomic adjustment generally benefits the poor.[8] Dismantling product and factor market rigidities helps reduce poverty by increasing not only the supply of essential goods, but also the poor's access to them.[9] In addition, based on cross-country studies, there is increasing evidence that lower inflation also enhances income equality (Milanovic, 1994; Bulír and Gulde, 1995; Sarel, 1997; Bulír, 1998; and Guitián, 1998).

Two Social Sector Issues

Nevertheless, in the short run, measures needed for macroeconomic stability can adversely affect some poor groups, while helping other such groups. For example, currency devaluations may hurt the urban poor who consume imported grains, while helping low-income smallholders producing export crops in rural areas. Mitigating the adverse effects of reform programs on poor groups should be an important aspect of the IMF's policy advice and program design.

The size and quality of public social spending can affect long-run growth and poverty reduction. The relationship between public social spending, growth, and poverty reduction, however, is complex and dynamic, involving many other factors, including private spending on education and health care. Forging a consensus on a proper balance between macroeconomic stabilization and sound public spending through a participatory dialogue among the government, civil society, and the international community can be facilitated by establishing social and poverty reduction programs that are integrated into a sustainable medium-term budgetary framework.

Key Steps in the Evolution

Over the years, the IMF has taken a progressively more active stance on social policies to ensure that they are well integrated into IMF-supported programs and IMF policy advice. The IMF has strengthened the integration of social policies into its operations by establishing the Structural Adjustment Facility (SAF) in 1986 and its successor, the Enhanced Structural Adjustment Facility (ESAF) in 1987, and the Initiative for Heavily Indebted Poor Countries (HIPCs) in 1996 (Box 2.1).[10]

A key element of these new instruments has been the collaborative role of the World Bank. The IMF and the World Bank have collaborated through the Policy Framework Paper (PFP) in the ESAF and through the joint HIPC Initiative. More broadly, the IMF has intensified collaboration with other international agencies that have social policy expertise. IMF staff has participated in international social policy forums relevant to the IMF's economic policy advice. For example, the staff contributed to the discussion at the 1995 World Summit for Social Development in

---

[6]As regards fiscal deficits, see Fischer (1991); Levine and Zervos (1993); Easterly and Rebelo (1993); Bredenkamp and Schadler (1999); and Goldsbrough and others (1996); as regards inflation, see Barro (1995); Bruno and Easterly (1995); Sarel (1996); and Ghosh and Phillips (1998). Macroeconomic stability—lower (and stable) inflation—has also been shown to be conducive to higher long-run growth (World Bank, 1996).

[7]World Bank (1996).

[8]Demery and Squire's (1996) review of six African countries has shown that macroeconomic adjustment has generally benefited the poor.

[9]Sahn, Dorosh, and Younger (1997), in a comprehensive study based on computable general equilibrium models of 10 sub-Saharan countries, concluded that under structural adjustment programs supported by the IMF and the World Bank, most of the poor experienced small net gains. They also showed that structural reforms hurt those reaping rents from distortionary policies, who tend to be nonpoor.

---

[10]See, for example, IMF (1995) and Gupta and others (1998).

Box 2.1. Evolution of the IMF's Social Policy Advice

Recent Evolution

Specific operational guidance has been provided to the staff of the IMF through Executive Board discussions and guidelines.

- In the mid-1980s, Board discussions were held on poverty, fiscal policy, and income distribution in IMF-supported programs.[1]

- In 1993, the Executive Board considered issues concerning the design of social safety nets and their integration in adjustment programs, and in the mid-1990s the composition of public expenditures.

- In September 1996, the Interim Committee (now the International Monetary and Financial Committee) stressed the need for an enhanced approach to social sector policies in a declaration entitled Partnership for Sustainable Growth. It states that "because the sustainability of economic growth depends on development of human resources, it is essential to improve education and training; to reform public pension and health systems to ensure their long-term viability and enable the provision of effective health care; and to alleviate poverty and provide well-targeted and affordable social safety nets."[2]

- In June 1997, guidelines for improving the monitoring of social expenditures and social indicators were issued to IMF staff. The social indicators to be monitored included the core set of international development goals and indicators laid out in the

March 1995 "Copenhagen Declaration on Social Development and Program of Action" of the World Summit for Social Development. Also, several of the recommendations of a recent external evaluation relating to the social aspects of the ESAF are being incorporated in ESAF-supported programs,[3] including through a pilot program for enhanced World Bank–IMF collaboration launched in 1998. Under this pilot program, World Bank and IMF staff work with six countries to make deeper assessments of the social impact of adjustment policies and to address these effects in the design of the countries' IMF-supported programs.

- More recently, especially in the aftermath of the Asian financial crisis, the Managing Director, Michel Camdessus, has stressed the need for a social pillar in the architecture of the international financial system.

Current Developments

- The World Bank was requested by the Development Committee in October 1998 to develop general principles of good practice in social policies, and a paper was discussed at the Spring 1999 Meeting of the Development Committee. The President of the World Bank, James Wolfensohn, has also proposed a Comprehensive Development Framework. A social pillar would need to be founded on a strong statement of social objectives by countries in their policy frameworks, supported when needed by external financial and technical assistance.

---

[1]See, for example, IMF (1996) and various Development Committee documents.
[2]See IMF (1996).

[3]See IMF (1997) and Abed and others (1998) for the internal review of ESAF.

Copenhagen and recently to UN/OECD/World Bank discussions on a core set of international development goals and indicators (Box 2.2). The IMF also has organized conferences on Income Distribution and Sustainable Growth (1995) and on Economic Policy and Equity (1998) (see Tanzi and Chu, 1998; and Tanzi, Chu, and Gupta, 1999). In addition, IMF

management and staff have engaged the representatives of civil society groups, including labor unions, NGOs, and religious groups, in a dialogue on social concerns and IMF policy advice. For example, meetings with such groups are now commonplace during staff missions or at headquarters.[11]

---

[11]Among the frequent contacts in civil society groups are Oxfam, Friends of the Earth, World Vision, the Swiss Council of Development Organizations, Witness for Peace, Christian Aid, Results International, and Caritas Internationalis. The IMF has organized numerous seminars for academics, labor unions, environmental groups, religious organizations, and development

NGOs. In 1996, the Managing Director addressed a World Congress of the International Confederation of Free Trade Unions (ICFTU) and in 1997 the World Conference of Labor. In addition, the IMF has greatly increased the dissemination of information through press releases, public information notes, and the publication of some staff reports and other studies.

Box 2.2. International Social Development Goals and Performance Indicators

Goals of Social Development

Since the early 1990s, various global UN conferences have established goals for social policies, as well as for the environment, human settlements, human rights, drug control, and crime prevention. In particular, the Copenhagen Declaration on Social Development (March 1995) laid out a program of action that, among other things, included the goals of eradicating poverty, promoting social integration, and achieving universal and equitable access to education and primary health care.

Key goals of social development are, by the year 2015, to

- reduce the proportion of people living in poverty by at least one-half relative to 1993;
- achieve universal primary education in all countries;
- make progress toward gender equality by eliminating gender disparity in primary and secondary education (to be achieved by 2005);
- reduce maternal mortality rates by three-fourths and reduce infant and child mortality rates by two-thirds relative to 1990; and
- provide access to reproductive health services to all individuals of appropriate ages.

Indicators for Measuring Progress

Several sets of social indicators have been identified in various forums to assess social development and monitor key social development goals. Examples of such sets of social indicators are

- the OECD/UN/World Bank core set of working indicators of international development goals;[1]
- the Common Country Assessment (CCA) indicators of the UN Development Assistance Framework (UNDAF);
- the UN/CCA Task Force on Basic Social Services for All (BSSA) indicators; and
- the UN Statistical Commission's Minimum National Social Data Set (MNSDS).[2]

The IMF has been supportive of these efforts.

The OECD, World Bank, and UN, in cooperation with developing countries and bilateral donors, have established the following working set of **core indicators on social development:**

- **Poverty:** share of the population living below $1 a day in purchasing power parity terms; the poverty gap (the resources needed to lift all those below the poverty line out of poverty); prevalence of underweight children under 5 years of age; and the share of the poorest 20 percent in national consumption.
- **Education:** net enrollment rates in primary education; completion rate of fourth grade of primary education; and literacy rate of those between 15 and 24 years of age.
- **Gender equality:** ratio of girls to boys in primary and secondary education; ratio of literate females to males (ages 15 to 24).
- **Health:** infant mortality rate; under-5 mortality rate; maternal mortality rate; percentage of births attended by skilled personnel; contraceptive prevalence rate; and HIV prevalence in pregnant women aged 15 to 24 (for lack of data, currently the overall HIV prevalence rate is used).

In addition, the OECD/UN/World Bank core list includes 6 environment indicators, as well as 10 background indicators of development, such as adult literacy rate, total fertility rate, and life expectancy.

The CCA/UNDAF list includes all indicators in the OECD/UN/World Bank core set, but for some development goals, the list has a more extensive scope, including, for example, more indicators on gender equality and women's empowerment, child welfare, and food security. In addition, the CCA/UNDAF list has indicators relating to employment, housing, drug control, and crime prevention.

Compared with the CCA/BSSA and MNSDS sets, the OECD/UN/World Bank list is more extensive and includes a wider range of social development indicators. However, the CCA/BSSA and MNSDS sets also include some indicators not found in the OECD/UN/World Bank list, such as average years of schooling (MNSDS) and access to primary health care services (BSSA).

All these sets are intended to be used flexibly, and need to be adapted to the specific circumstances of the country to which they are applied. Indicators may be added if they capture an aspect of social development not included in the sets, while lack of data may require that some indicators be omitted.

_____

[1]Available via the Internet: http://www.oecd.org/dac/indicators/htm/tables.htm.

[2]These indicators and their definitions are available in the World Bank's World Development Indicators database and in the UN Development Program's (UNDP) *Human Development Reports,* which are available via the Internet: http://www.undp.org/hdro/indicators.html#developing.

III Social Safety Nets

In countries where the authorities could foresee that reform measures would have a sizable adverse social impact, the policy mix and sequencing have aimed to take this impact into account within a sustainable macroeconomic framework. For instance, IMF-supported programs have aimed to phase out subsidies for food and other items gradually, rather than at once (e.g., Indonesia, 1998; and Senegal, 1994–95). The adverse impact, however, cannot be totally eliminated even with an appropriate policy mix and sequencing. For instance, a change in relative prices that hurts the poor—such as a devaluation that could adversely effect the urban poor through increasing prices of imported products—may be at the heart of a reform program. A tension may emerge, therefore, between stabilization and social protection objectives.

Social safety nets are a means of easing this tension. IMF staff—drawing on the work of other institutions—has increasingly sought to incorporate social safety nets into adjustment programs. The IMF's Executive Board, following its discussion of social safety nets in 1993, endorsed this approach.[12] More recently, ESAF-supported programs have sought larger budget allocations for social safety nets. There has been an increase in the use of structural benchmarks and performance criteria aimed at securing social protection objectives (Box 3.1).

This review indicates that most IMF-supported programs have incorporated social safety nets, although there is scope for further improvement in their quality and implementation.

- The social safety nets in IMF-supported programs have included new temporary arrangements—such as temporary subsidies and public works programs—as well as existing social protection instruments adapted to the needs of target groups—such as pensions and other permanent social security programs (see Chu and Gupta, 1998). Measures designed to foster financial stability, such as the adoption of deposit guarantees (limited or general) and other financial restructuring measures to maximize asset recoveries, to redistribute losses, and to sustain credit to the small and medium-sized industry segments, also have protected small depositors and vulnerable groups.

- Over time, permanent social protection arrangements (e.g., pensions, unemployment insurance) also have been established in the context of reform programs.

- Family-based safety nets have cushioned income losses during adjustment periods in many countries. For example, in Indonesia, in the wake of the recent crisis, about a fourth of families received informal transfers (Frankenberg, Thomas, and Beegle, 1999). Such informal arrangements have been generally well targeted.[13] Thus the design of public social safety nets has sought to avoid duplicating the system of voluntary, private transfers.

The timely implementation of social safety nets has been hampered—all too frequently—by a lack of existing social policy instruments. Often these instruments can be speedily adapted to the needs of the new target groups. But sometimes the adaptation is difficult. Countries often have not had the will to reform costly existing social protection mechanisms or to shift social protection priorities. Those segments of the population suffering from the adverse effects of reforms may prove to be different from those protected by the permanent arrangements. In addition, the lack of data and administrative and financial constraints have hampered implementation and monitoring.

In most cases, IMF staff has relied largely on the World Bank, and regional development banks to

---

[12]The two conferences on income distribution and economic policy organized by the IMF in recent years have also emphasized the need for cost-effective social safety nets during reform periods. See Tanzi and Chu (1998) and Tanzi, Chu, and Gupta (1999).

[13]See Cox, Okrasa, and Jimenez (1997) and Cox, Eser, and Jimenez (1997) for such networks in Poland and the Russian Federation, respectively.

Box 3.1.   Strengthening Social Safety Nets in ESAF-Supported Programs, 1994–98

Policy Framework Papers (PFPs) and Memoranda of Economic Policies (MEPs) for 44 countries that had ESAF-supported programs during 1994–98 were reviewed to ascertain what kind of measures had been incorporated in programs to mitigate the adverse social effects of structural adjustment policies. These measures were classified into two groups:

- Budgetary allocations (either unspecified general allocations or quantitative commitments); and
- Measures to strengthen social protection through more specific targeting, better monitoring of the affected population groups, widened coverage of safety net measures, or related reforms.

A significant group of countries have incorporated allocations for social safety nets in their ESAF-supported programs, and the use of structural benchmarks and performance criteria for achieving social protection goals has grown.

- Half the countries had commitments in their PFPs for allocations for financing social safety nets during the program period (on average 3–3½ years), with a third of the 44 countries setting these targets in quantitative terms. During the review period, countries also included measures for strengthening the design and coverage of social safety nets; some established targets for the number of vulnerable people to be shielded by social safety nets (Armenia, Guyana, the Kyrgyz Republic, Mozambique, and Nicaragua).
- About three-fourths of countries announced spending on social safety nets in their MEPs during the program period, with 60 percent of the 44 countries specifying quantitative allocations. In recent years, however, the use of quantitative targets with respect to social safety nets has declined. A similar

trend is noticeable in the listing of structural measures for strengthening social safety nets. Although it is difficult to pinpoint the reasons for this trend, there are several possibilities. Priorities in programs could have shifted; the monitoring of social safety nets could have become more difficult because of data and other constraints; and in a number of countries, structural reforms with the greatest adverse social impact could have been felt earlier in the program periods. On a country-by-country basis, significantly fewer countries (about one-half) that sought allocations of expenditures on social safety nets in PFPs made the same commitments in their MEPs. Nine countries specified targets for the number of vulnerable to be shielded by social safety nets in MEPs (Albania, Armenia, the Republic of Congo, Haiti, the Kyrgyz Republic, the former Yugoslav Republic of Macedonia, Mozambique, Nicaragua, and Yemen).

Greater use of structural benchmarks and performance criteria for social safety nets in ESAF countries is a recent phenomenon. Structural benchmarks have included, for example, improving the transparency of energy subsidies, replacing generalized subsidies with targeted subsidies, and establishing labor retrenchment funds. Programs for six countries incorporated benchmarks (Azerbaijan in 1996, Cameroon in 1998, the Kyrgyz Republic in 1994, 1995, and 1998, the former Yugoslav Republic of Macedonia in 1997 and 1998, Pakistan in 1995–98, and Yemen in 1997–98). Of these, two countries have included performance criteria for achieving social protection objectives, for example, by strengthening the revenue position and by reforming the benefit structure of the employment and the pension funds (the Kyrgyz Republic in 1994, 1997, and 1998, and the former Yugoslav Republic of Macedonia in 1998).

---

some extent, to take the lead in the design of social safety nets for IMF-supported programs.

- For example, in Indonesia, a targeted rice subsidy and community-based public works programs, designed by the World Bank, were incorporated in the 1998 IMF-supported adjustment program. This was also the case for the public works programs financed by the Asian Development Bank and the World Bank in Thailand in 1998. In Brazil in 1999, the Inter-American Development Bank and the World Bank cofinanced a special adjustment loan for a social protection project that was integrated into the IMF-supported program.
- In some cases, the IMF Fiscal Affairs Department has provided limited technical assistance on social safety nets (e.g., Ecuador and Belarus

in 1999). And in 1999, the African Department recruited two social policy specialists with backgrounds in sociology to assist the department in incorporating appropriate social safety nets in countries' adjustment programs. To the extent possible, IMF missions have built on the work of the World Bank, regional development banks, other UN agencies, and NGOs.[14] In many cases, program-related missions have also focused on social issues.

---

[14]This approach is consistent with that set forth in the 1993 Development Committee paper prepared jointly by the staffs of the IMF and the World Bank. Executive Directors in the 1993 discussion on safety nets "agreed that the IMF's policy advice through technical assistance on social safety nets should be continued to the extent that staff resources were available."

Design Issues

The design of social safety nets has been influenced, among other things, by the availability of existing social policy instruments. For example, transition economies had a broad range of social instruments that were poorly targeted (e.g., Moldova and Ukraine). A wide range of benefits covered the bulk of the population, including the nonpoor. Thus the principal aim of IMF-supported programs in these countries has been to make spending—for instance, food subsidies—better targeted, rather than to create new instruments. In contrast, low-income developing countries had few and limited social policy instruments; the effort there has been to create arrangements that could reach affected groups, such as transitory subsidies for the urban poor in the CFA franc zone countries in the aftermath of the 1994 devaluation. In general, establishing cost-effective social safety nets would have been easier had well-targeted social policy instruments been already in place before the onset of crises and economic reforms.[15]

The specific adverse effects on and characteristics of target groups have determined the types of social safety net instruments.

- A sharp fall in output, reinforced by a large increase in prices of important staples, can result in a significant real income loss for those poor households who are net consumers of food. This occurred in Indonesia in 1998 and in transition economies in the initial stages of transformation. In these circumstances, income transfers or targeted food subsidies became critical.

- When the prices of essential goods rose in countries where the elderly constituted a high proportion of the population, low-income pensioners needed to be helped through an adequate minimum allowance (e.g., the Russian Federation and Ukraine).

- When there were regional pockets of unemployment, special programs to supplement incomes have been implemented (e.g., community-based public works programs in Indonesia and Senegal).

Nevertheless, the selection of target groups has raised fairness issues. To ensure political support for reform, social safety nets have been extended to politically vocal middle-income groups: for example, a subsidy for premium gasoline (in Indonesia, initially in 1998), severance payments for departing civil servants (Ghana and Lao People's Democratic Repub-

lic) and for public enterprise employees (Argentina and Bolivia), and food subsidies (Jordan). Unemployment benefits—largely for formal sector beneficiaries—were strengthened in the presence of a large informal sector, where the majority of the poor may be residing (Brazil in 1998).

To identify target groups, IMF staff has generally relied on the national authorities and the World Bank, which have provided a measure of the poverty line and household expenditure survey data on household characteristics.[16] The latter, however, are often conducted infrequently, with results that are not always timely or comparable across time.[17] Because of these constraints, poverty lines and poverty profiles have typically been unavailable for the year when reform programs were put in place (e.g., Brazil and Thailand).

The weak administrative capacity in many countries has hampered the targeting of benefits, particularly on the basis of incomes. This has meant a greater reliance on programs that have self-targeting features, such as

- public works with below-market wages (e.g., Indonesia, Malawi, Thailand, and Senegal);

- subsidies on commodities consumed by the poor (e.g., inferior rice in Indonesia); and

- shielding of groups that are easily identified as poor (pensioners, the unemployed, single mothers, and children).

Means testing based on wage income has been used in some countries—for the housing subsidy program in Ukraine, for example—but this carries the risk of mistargeting, especially in countries with a large informal sector, and could create disincentives for the supply of labor.

Financial constraints have limited the scope of social safety nets. The need to redress macroeconomic imbalances has typically precluded increasing total public spending; thus, a reallocation within the existing budgetary envelope to better-targeted programs has been necessary (e.g., Brazil).

- In some cases, such as Venezuela, eliminating subsidies has freed resources for more targeted social protection programs.

- Significant budgetary savings have often been achieved by reforming social safety nets, such

---

[15]Ferreira, Prennushi, and Ravallion (1999).

[16]The Poverty Assessments prepared by the World Bank have been particularly useful. In some cases, the World Bank and national authorities use different poverty lines (e.g., Belarus). In the design of social safety nets, the usual practice has been to use country-specific poverty lines, rather than international poverty lines defined in terms of U.S. dollars in purchasing power parity terms for daily consumption of an individual.

[17]Less than two-thirds of countries with IMF-supported programs have conducted at least one household or demographic survey, of which the last one in more than half of the countries was conducted before 1996.

Box 3.2. Social Safety Nets: Issues in Transition Economies

Key Issues

Transition economies have been trying to reform expansive, but increasingly ineffective, social protection arrangements, including subsidies, pensions, unemployment benefits, and family allowances. Declining taxes and social contributions have severely weakened the ability of many transition economies to provide the needed benefits.

- The declining social contributions have transformed the earnings-related pensions and other social benefits into virtually flat minimum benefits.

- Offsetting tax obligations of enterprises against obligations of the government has limited the ability of many governments to pay cash benefits. Moreover, these obligations of the government do not necessarily represent spending of high social value.

In many transition economies, the benefits have yet to be fully reformed.

- In Moldova, the Russian Federation, and Ukraine, pension systems have allowed workers to collect benefits at a relatively young age, and workers in certain occupations have been eligible for pensions even earlier. Pensions have been based not only on the number of years of contributions, but also on years spent studying or taking care of a young child.

- A large part of social contributions collected for assisting the unemployed continue to be wasted on low-priority programs and benefits administration;

only a small share of the unemployed actually receive assistance in any form.

- Traditional extensive and generous privileges for politically influential groups (judges, parliamentarians, internal security personnel) prevent the targeting of limited resources to the genuinely needy.

IMF Advice

Thus, the emphasis of IMF staff advice has been on improving compliance with tax laws, simplifying the rate structure, and stopping the collection of taxes and social contributions in kind (e.g., Azerbaijan, Moldova, and Ukraine). Some progress in simplifying the social contribution rate structure has been made, but significant change in other areas has been elusive.

In these and other similar cases, IMF staff have called for raising the pension age, eliminating privileged and early pensions and untargeted benefits, targeting social assistance and subsidies, increasing the size and coverage of unemployment benefits, and making social benefits more transparent. Pension reforms are under consideration in many transition countries, but the progress in implementing far-reaching reforms remains slow. For example, despite the emphasis given to pension reform, including the use of performance criteria, in IMF-supported programs in the Kyrgyz Republic, relatively little progress was achieved; a concerted and more comprehensive and resource-intensive World Bank adjustment operation appears to have had more success in pension reform since 1998.

---

as by replacing generalized subsidies with targeted ones (e.g., rice subsidies in Indonesia).

- External donors, including the World Bank, have played a role in some cases, in particular by funding severance payments for departing civil servants and by providing food aid (e.g., Senegal).

- In transition countries, the large decline in output has increased the demand for social benefits while reducing the availability of financing (Box 3.2).

When the adverse impact exceeded expectations, program targets have been changed to accommodate larger budgetary outlays for social safety nets. Indonesia, Korea, and Thailand raised spending on social protection programs to 5.2 percent of GDP in 1998/99, 2 percent of GDP in 1999, and 2 percent of GDP in 1998/99, respectively, from between 1/2 percent and 1 percent of GDP in each country before the crisis.

In general, and beyond the context of immediate program requirements, it would be desirable to identify the need for social policy instruments and advise government authorities to seek necessary assistance from the World Bank and others, in the course of IMF surveillance. Such efforts could, among other things, speed the establishment of cost-effective safety nets if difficulties arise and reform measures need to be undertaken.

Labor Market Implications

Labor market incentives have been a key concern in the design of unemployment benefits. The challenge has been to strike an appropriate balance between social protection and disincentive effects, although, certainly, this balance may differ among countries, depending on social preferences, norms, and other factors. In 1998, because of their concerns about possible disincentive effects, the Korean authorities initially hesitated to broaden the coverage of unemployment benefits. A relatively high wage for participants of public works programs can undermine their effectiveness as a safety net by attracting already employed workers.[18]

Establishing social safety nets, however, can help promote a fundamental labor market reform. Before the financial crisis in 1997, lifelong employment in large enterprises had been an important aspect of social protection in Korea. But it constrained the ability of enterprises to restructure in the face of changing economic conditions. Broadening the coverage of unemployment benefits to 70 percent of the labor force in early 1999 from around 30 percent supported labor market reform aimed at promoting labor market flexibility by providing income transfers to those switching jobs.

Monitoring

The staff monitoring of social safety nets has been infrequent. A review of 12 countries[19] with ESAF arrangements during 1994–98 indicates that, although over three-fourths of Policy Framework Papers (PFPs) and Memoranda of Economic Policies (MEPs) reported on the performance of social safety nets under IMF-supported programs, such monitoring typically occurred only once or twice. The infrequent monitoring of social safety nets may have reflected weak national capacity to monitor the implementation of social policies and their impact on poverty.

The staff's assessment and reporting of the effectiveness of social safety nets have been uneven. In only a third of the 12 countries reviewed did staff papers assess the coverage and incidence of social safety nets during the five-year period (e.g., with respect to temporary food subsidies and to fertilizer provision to smallholders in Malawi). For a larger number of countries (more than three-fourths), staff papers reported on the improvements in the benefit structure and financing of social protection mechanisms. In contrast, staff papers on IMF-supported programs for the countries affected by the recent crisis in Asia (Indonesia, Korea, and Thailand) reported extensively on social safety net developments.[20]

---

[18]The wages paid to participants are the most critical determinant of overall program cost and the effectiveness of job creation through public works schemes. Experience from a range of countries shows that programs are more effective when the wage is maintained at a level below the prevailing market wage for unskilled labor. See Subbarao and others (1997).

[19]Azerbaijan, Bolivia, Georgia, Guyana, the Kyrgyz Republic, the Lao People's Democratic Republic, the former Yugoslav

---

Republic of Macedonia, Malawi, Mongolia, Pakistan, Senegal, and Vietnam.

[20]With the support of the World Bank, a few countries have recently established a mechanism to monitor social outcomes on an ongoing basis (e.g., the Social Monitoring and Early Response Unit in Indonesia).

IV Public Spending on Education and Health Care

The relationship between public social spending, social indicators, and poverty reduction is complex and dynamic. How much public social spending reduces poverty depends not only on the amount allocated for education and health care, but also on how efficiently these allocations are spent and how well they are targeted to the poor.[21] Education and health care indicators are affected not only by government outlays on education and health care but also by private spending, demographic trends, and public spending in other areas such as sanitation and safe water. Empirical research on the link between increased aggregate public spending on education and health care and improvements in related social indicators has yielded conflicting evidence.[22] Note, also, that today's illiteracy and infant mortality rates are normally the result of yesterday's social policies; poverty reduction reflects past increases in spending on primary education, primary school enrollment, and literacy. Finally, some indicators reflect *intermediate* outputs, not final outcomes. For example, widespread immunization of infants under 12 months against measles does not by itself yield a low infant mortality rate, especially if other variables, such as access to safe water and female education attainment, are relatively poorly developed.[23]

This review suggests that considerable progress has been achieved in strengthening spending policies on public education and health care, but that some areas require further efforts.

- Countries have made considerable progress in establishing comprehensive and structured policy frameworks for such spending; more recently, there have been discernible improvements in targeting and monitoring public spending and positive, albeit modest, developments in related social indicators and outcomes.

- Efforts to raise spending on education and health care have achieved relatively more success in the HIPC decision point countries (Bolivia, Burkina Faso, Côte d'Ivoire, Mozambique, and Uganda) than in other IMF-supported program countries.

Further improvements, however, are needed to address some inadequacies:

- Lack of adequate data is commonplace. Data on the composition of education and health care spending are often not available. Data on subnational government spending are scarce. Education and health achievement indicators are either unavailable or available with a long lag (Box 4.1).

- Policy objectives have not always been clear or articulated in terms of well-defined targets against which progress can be measured, and the definition of targets and monitoring often has changed over time within a single country.

The HIPC Initiative framework has yielded relatively more progress than have other programs, across a more comprehensive range of social sector reforms. The most marked improvements in social indicators during the period under review also have taken place in HIPC countries. No causal association, however, can be established between increased spending and outcomes, because their link is affected by many other factors.

Aggregate Spending on Education and Health Care

IMF-supported programs have sought to promote universal access to basic social services. Programs have increased public spending for such services in countries where this spending was low, supported high-quality expenditure in these sectors, and pro-

---

[21]There are wide disparities in the cost-effectiveness of government spending on education and health care across countries in Africa, and, in general, these countries were found to be less efficient than those in the Western Hemisphere and Asia. See Gupta, Verhoeven, and Honjo (1997).

[22]See Mingat and Tan (1998); Filmer, Hammer, and Pritchett (1998); and Gupta, Verhoeven, and Tiongson (1999).

[23]For example, for the latest year for which data are available, Zambia has a higher immunization coverage than Kenya, but also a higher infant mortality rate. In contrast, for a group of 48 program countries for which recent data are available, there is a negative and statistically significant correlation between immunization coverage and infant mortality rate.

Box 4.1. Quality of Social Spending and Indicators Data

Social Spending

Many deficiencies exist in data on public spending on education and health care.

- In general, spending by local governments is not included; this can be a major handicap in countries that have devolved or are devolving expenditure responsibilities to lower levels of the government, particularly those related to basic education.

- In many cases, data coverage in fiscal accounts is limited to current outlays, in part owing to the inability of governments to separate donor-financed capital spending by function.

- In-kind donor contributions to education and health care are not included.

- Data typically become available with a lag, which for some countries can be as long as two to three years.

- Virtually no country has consistent annual series for expenditure allocations *within* the education and health care sectors (e.g., separating between primary and tertiary education, or preventive health care and curative health care), and the data available in many cases are not consistent with aggregate fiscal data.

- Despite the importance of books and medicine for developments in social indicators, separate data for nonwage and wage outlays in education and health care sectors are available for only very few countries.

- Data on private sector outlays on education and health care are not collected on a regular basis.

Social Indicators

The most serious shortcoming of data on social indicators is that they are generally produced infrequently and with a long lag, or, in many cases, are not collected at all. For instance, data for 1997 are available for only 11 out of 18 indicators of well-being and social development in the working set identified by the OECD/UN/World Bank, and only for a small number of developing and transition countries. Current data for many important indicators are derived from models, rather than from actual observations. For example, for 102 countries, actual observations on infant mortality rates are not available for 1985 or later.

Furthermore, some of the key indicators become available only every five years. In some cases, there is a trade-off between the availability of data on social indicators and their quality. For instance, net enrollment rates, which correct for grade repetition, are available for only about half of program countries, whereas gross enrollment rates, which are available for most countries, count all students regardless of age as part of the school-going population, thus overstating enrollment to the extent students are repeating grades (see Table 4.1). There may also be inconsistencies among data sources and compilation methods, raising questions about data comparability across countries and over time. Because indicators are constructed by using data collected at the national level through censuses, sample surveys, and administrative records, data quality to a large extent depends on the national statistical capacity.

---

tected or sought real increases in these expenditures during adjustment periods when poor households might lack the ability to pay for basic social services. The importance programs have attached to these objectives was reflected in the increasing use of quantitative targets, structural benchmarks, and performance criteria aimed at raising education and health care spending (Box 4.2).[24]

Overall, considerable progress was made in increasing social spending during 1985–97. Although the lack of consistent data hinders the assessment of public social spending, program countries, on average, have achieved an increase in social spending:

- For 65 of the 107 countries with IMF-supported programs during 1985–97, government spending on education and health care, on average, has increased both as a percentage of GDP and in real per capita terms. The share in GDP of spending increased by 0.3 percentage point during the program period (about eight years, on average); the spending increased by 2.4 percent a year in real per capita terms (Figure 4.1).[25]

- In a subset of 29 countries, of which 19 are ESAF countries, that have data on military spending, such spending on average declined during 1990–97, whereas education and health care spending together increased in relation to both GDP and total government spending.

---

[24]Notwithstanding the problems with comparability, IMF staff have compiled cross-country data on public education and health care spending. This data set covers 65 countries that are implementing or have implemented IMF-supported reform programs, of which 31 are low-income countries with ESAF-supported programs. The GDP deflator was used to convert nominal expenditures into real terms. In principle, deflating by public sector wages would provide a more accurate reading of real trends in education and health care spending. But such wage data are rarely available for low-income countries. In 10 countries in Africa for which data on public sector wages are available, real per capita spending on education and health care increased, on average, by 2 percent a year under IMF-supported programs—a result consistent with spending trends derived from the GDP deflator.

[25]See Gupta, Verhoeven, Yamada, and Tiongson (1999).

Box 4.2.   Targets for Public Spending on Education and Health Care in ESAF-Supported Programs, 1994–98

Policy Framework Papers (PFPs) as well as Memoranda of Economic Policies (MEPs) for 44 countries that had ESAF-supported programs during 1994–98 were reviewed to ascertain the extent to which they

- incorporated targets for budget allocations for education and health care, either in unspecified general or specific quantitative terms;
- called for structural improvements in the provision of social services; and
- monitored changes in, and established targets for, social indicators.

ESAF-supported programs have increasingly sought to raise public spending on education and health care and to implement structural reforms in the sectors. Benchmarks and performance criteria have also been increasingly widely used to achieve increases in such spending.

In PFPs, about 80 percent of the 44 countries sought increases in public spending on education and health care during 1994–98, and a slightly lower proportion (60 percent) set quantitative targets for such increases. Targets were most commonly set once during the period while, on average, ESAF-supported programs were in place in the countries for 3–3½ years during 1994–98. PFPs for around 60 percent of the 44 countries aimed at increased budgetary allocations for primary education and basic health care during the period, and about one-third of these set quantitative increases. All programs called for structural measures to strengthen the provision of social services during the period, for example, by increasing the number of teachers and doctors and enhancing the role of the private sector. About 45 percent of the 44 countries targeted improvements in social indicators in both unspecified and quantitative terms. The most commonly used indicators were primary school enrollment, including, separately for girls, literacy, infant mortality, and immunization rates.

The picture is broadly similar for MEPs with respect to the proportion of countries that committed to increase budgetary expenditures on health care and education. Compared with PFPs, however, a much smaller percentage of countries (about 45 percent) sought increases in budgetary allocations for primary education and basic health care (either unspecified or in specific quantitative terms) and some 16 percent established specific targets for quantitative increases. A lower percentage of countries (30 percent) identified improvements in education and health care indicators as a policy objective. The use of quantitative targets increased by 40 percent during the period under review.

On a country-by-country basis, commitments to social spending measures were less frequent in MEPs than in PFPs. For example, only about half the countries that sought increases in social expenditures in their PFPs mentioned such increases in the MEPs.

In recent years, programs have relied on benchmarks and performance criteria to seek increases in, and strengthen the efficiency of, social spending. To this end, the MEPs of six countries included benchmarks (Armenia in 1996, Azerbaijan in 1997, Cameroon in 1997, Georgia in 1997 and 1998, the Kyrgyz Republic in 1995, 1997, and 1998, and Uganda in 1997), and two countries included performance criteria (Ghana in 1998 and the Kyrgyz Republic in 1998).

- Real per capita social spending has declined in some countries, and the increases have been relatively low in some regions, notably education spending in sub-Saharan Africa.[26] In transition economies, real per capita spending on education and health care has declined considerably. A modest decline of 0.1 of a percentage point in the share of spending in falling GDP masks a larger decline in real per capita terms. In these countries, however, education and health care spending have been historically high and inefficient.

- Countries with ESAF-supported programs have shown relatively strong results. In the 31 countries with ESAF programs, the real per capita growth of spending on education and health care over 1985–97 (4.0 percent and 4.9 percent, respectively) has outstripped, on average, that in other program countries.

In 1997, public expenditure on education and health care as a share of GDP in countries with ESAF programs approximated that in other program countries. In HIPCs, spending levels remain below those in other program countries in part because of very low initial levels (Figure 4.2). Educa-

---

[26]The countries where spending on education as a share of GDP declined are the Republic of Congo, Côte d'Ivoire, Guinea-Bissau, Madagascar, Mali, Mozambique, and Nigeria. In health care, the Comoros, Guinea-Bissau, Nigeria, and Zambia experienced a decline in spending as a percentage of GDP. The countries where real per capita spending on education declined are the Comoros, Côte d'Ivoire, the Republic of Congo, Kenya, Madagascar, Mali, Nigeria, and Sierra Leone. In part, this reflected cuts in salary from a high level (e.g., Côte d'Ivoire). In health care, the countries where real per capita spending on health care declined are the Comoros, Côte d'Ivoire, Kenya, Madagascar, Nigeria, and Zambia.

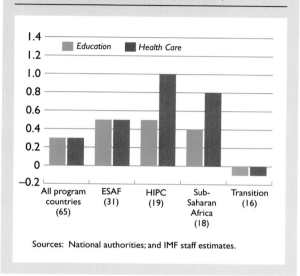

Figure 4.1. Changes in Education and Health Care Spending in Countries with IMF-Supported Programs, 1985–97
(Average change between preprogram year and latest year in percent of GDP; number of countries in parentheses)

Sources: National authorities; and IMF staff estimates.

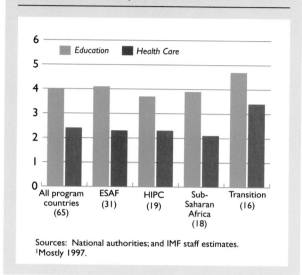

Figure 4.2. Spending Levels on Education and Health Care in Countries with IMF-Supported Programs, 1997
(In percent of GDP; number of countries in parentheses; latest year for which data are available)[1]

Sources: National authorities; and IMF staff estimates.
[1]Mostly 1997.

tion and health care spending as a share of total government spending—indicative of the priority assigned to these types of spending—shows the same pattern.

Composition of Spending

Available data for 1985–97 suggest that budget expenditure shares shifted, on average, from current to capital outlays in both ESAF countries and HIPCs, and more so than in other program countries. Whether this led to an increase in such key components in the delivery of education and health care as books and medicine, however, is unclear because available data for these outlays are reported with other types of spending under other goods and services. In all program countries, average spending on other goods and services fell during the period under review.

Although many programs have sought to improve the allocation of budget resources within the education and health care sectors, more can be done. On average, program countries have devoted a relatively large share of their education budget to tertiary education and even a larger part of health care outlays to curative services (Figure 4.3). This suggests that low-income households would benefit from a shift in budgetary resources toward primary education and basic health care.[27]

Impact on Education and Health Indicators and Implications for Poverty

On average, the education and health care indicators in the OECD/UN/World Bank working set of core indicators for measuring social development have improved for program countries.[28] But there are important exceptions. In sub-Saharan Africa, average life expectancy has declined, reflecting the toll of HIV and conflicts (Table 4.1). Improvements in social indicators in ESAF countries and HIPCs have not been commensurate with the spending increases. Progress in improving infant mortality and primary and secondary enrollment has been slower in these countries than in other program countries. Transition economies have experienced declines in enrollment rates in secondary education and immunizations; reforms in these two areas have been slow, thus increasing the risk that the declines in spending may lead to a permanent setback in social indicators.[29]

---

[27]See World Bank (1993 and 1995); and Gupta, Verhoeven, and Tiongson (1999).

[28]As yet, there is no consensus in international forums on the precise social indicators to be used for assessing development and social performance. As noted in Box 2.2, there are at present four sets of indicators in use.

[29]For a discussion of the reasons for the slow pace of reforms in education and health care spending in transition countries, see Gupta (1998).

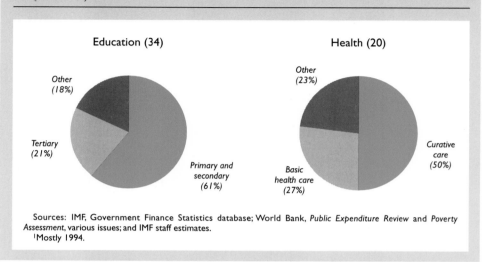

Figure 4.3. Allocation of Education and Health Care Spending in Countries with IMF-Supported Programs, 1994

(In percent of total education and health care spending; number of countries in parentheses; latest year for which data are available)[1]

Education (34)

Other (18%)

Tertiary (21%)

Primary and secondary (61%)

Health (20)

Other (23%)

Basic health care (27%)

Curative care (50%)

Sources: IMF, Government Finance Statistics database; World Bank, *Public Expenditure Review* and *Poverty Assessment*, various issues; and IMF staff estimates.
[1]Mostly 1994.

Weak administrative capacity to formulate and execute the budget has reduced the impact of education and health care spending on social indicators. In particular, the capacity to spend resources efficiently can vary at different levels of government, and is likely to be lacking at lower levels of government, at least initially, during a period of devolution of expenditure responsibilities.[30] The allocation of budgetary resources within the social sectors (e.g., between primary and tertiary education) is also important, as is the presence of corruption, which can distort the composition and level of social spending.[31]

Although improvements in social indicators reflect a country's social development, they have not been necessarily translated into reduced poverty, which in itself is multidimensional. For example, the poor tend to be less educated and less healthy than the nonpoor.[32] For targeted spending to have a considerable payoff, however, *the benefits from improved basic social services have to be accompanied by income-earning opportunities.*

Data for 29 program countries show that the targeting of education and health care spending could be improved, particularly in sub-Saharan Africa and in the transition economies (Figure 4.4). The poor's access may be constrained by out-of-pocket costs (both formal and informal) for using public services, excessive distance to the nearest school or health center, poor quality of public services, and gender bias. For sub-Saharan Africa,

- 14 percent of total spending on public education and 12 percent of health care spending, on average, accrue to the poorest fifth (quintile) of households compared with 30 percent for the richest quintile for both. These gaps widen for spending on secondary and tertiary education and hospital care;

- spending on primary education is somewhat better targeted than that on secondary and tertiary education, and the targeting of public spending on education and health care is improving in some countries (e.g., Côte d'Ivoire and Malawi).

Targeting has a geographical dimension. For example, government public policy choices with a pro-urban bias reduce the access to vital social services for the poor, most of whom live in rural areas. Data on the geographic distribution of education spending were available for only 10 countries with IMF-supported programs, and show that education spending, on average, has disproportionately favored the urban population, particularly spending on secondary and tertiary

---

[30]This has been an issue during the decentralization of government in Ethiopia; see Ter-Minassian (1997, Chapter 20).

[31]For example, if budget allocations in the health sector are made on the basis of the number of beds in a hospital, hospital administrators and doctors may increase the number of beds and keep them occupied, squeezing allocations for medicine. See also Tanzi (1998) and Mauro (1998).

[32]See Anand and Ravallion (1993) and Bidani and Ravallion (1997).

Table 4.1. Improvement in Social Indicators in Member Countries, 1985–97
(Current level and average annual percent improvement; number of countries in parentheses)

	Current Level[1]			Average Annual Percent Improvement							
	Non-program countries[2]	Program countries	ESAF program countries only	Non-program countries[2]	Program countries	ESAF program countries only	HIPC countries only	Sub-Saharan Africa	Asia and the Pacific	Latin America and the Caribbean	Transition economies
Education											
Illiteracy rate[3]	15.8 (22)	27.4 (49)	45.5 (21)	3.4 (22)	3.5 (49)	2.2 (21)	2.2 (16)	2.4 (15)	3.1 (8)	2.9 (14)	7.9 (7)
Female	18.6 (22)	32.8 (49)	53.4 (21)	3.6 (22)	3.5 (49)	2.1 (21)	2.0 (16)	2.3 (15)	3.1 (8)	3.0 (14)	8.3 (7)
Gross primary school enrollment rate[4]	104.2 (25)	92.3 (55)	80.9 (25)	0.1 (25)	0.8 (55)	1.0 (25)	0.9 (15)	0.6 (15)	0.5 (10)	0.7 (14)	1.0 (13)
Female	102.8 (25)	88.6 (52)	76.6 (24)	0.3 (25)	0.8 (52)	1.1 (24)	1.2 (14)	1.1 (14)	1.4 (9)	0.5 (13)	0.1 (13)
Male	105.8 (25)	96.5 (52)	88.0 (24)	0.1 (25)	0.7 (52)	0.9 (24)	1.4 (14)	1.0 (14)	0.0 (9)	0.6 (13)	0.8 (13)
Gross secondary school enrollment rate[4]	61.8 (25)	50.5 (53)	30.6 (24)	2.8 (25)	1.1 (53)	0.8 (24)	0.9 (14)	1.2 (14)	2.2 (10)	1.4 (14)	-0.8 (12)
Female	65.0 (24)	49.5 (49)	28.4 (23)	3.2 (24)	1.9 (49)	2.3 (23)	2.8 (13)	3.1 (14)	3.5 (10)	1.2 (10)	-0.5 (12)
Male	62.6 (24)	51.9 (49)	32.5 (23)	2.7 (24)	0.6 (49)	0.2 (23)	0.5 (13)	0.3 (14)	1.6 (10)	1.4 (10)	-0.9 (12)
Net primary school enrollment rate	84.8 (18)	74.6 (31)	58.9 (17)	0.2 (18)	0.7 (31)	0.6 (17)	0.5 (11)	0.1 (10)	0.9 (4)	0.9 (11)	0.4 (4)
Persistence to grade 5	88.5 (21)	75.3 (23)	68.0 (11)	0.5 (21)	1.7 (23)	2.0 (11)	2.9 (8)	2.3 (9)	-0.3 (5)	2.5 (7)	... (0)
Health care											
Life expectancy (in years)	68.1 (33)	63.3 (45)	57.6 (25)	0.4 (33)	0.2 (45)	0.2 (25)	0.1 (12)	-0.1 (13)	0.7 (4)	0.5 (9)	0.0 (16)
Infant mortality rate[3]	31.8 (34)	48.9 (48)	72.8 (25)	1.7 (34)	2.5 (48)	1.5 (25)	1.6 (13)	1.0 (14)	2.7 (5)	3.3 (10)	3.0 (16)
Under-5 mortality rate[3]	40.1 (29)	66.6 (29)	113.2 (14)	3.8 (29)	3.7 (29)	2.9 (14)	2.3 (8)	0.8 (8)	... (0)	3.2 (7)	5.7 (13)
Births attended by skilled staff	78.5 (25)	64.0 (37)	52.4 (18)	6.1 (25)	1.8 (37)	3.2 (18)	0.8 (10)	1.7 (9)	4.2 (10)	-0.1 (11)	-0.3 (4)
Contraceptive prevalence[5]	66.3 (4)	49.3 (14)	36.0 (5)	3.6 (4)	3.1 (14)	5.6 (5)	6.7 (3)	6.9 (3)	2.0 (5)	2.5 (5)	0.0 (1)
Access to health care	94.6 (16)	74.0 (13)	48.7 (3)	1.4 (16)	3.7 (13)	11.2 (3)	4.0 (4)	6.6 (5)	6.2 (2)	0.4 (4)	... (0)
Percent under 12 months immunized DPT vaccination	86.8 (33)	82.6 (61)	74.6 (29)	4.5 (33)	4.8 (61)	6.9 (29)	7.3 (16)	5.7 (15)	7.7 (10)	3.8 (15)	3.7 (16)
Measles vaccination	85.0 (33)	83.0 (60)	75.3 (28)	5.4 (33)	4.4 (60)	6.1 (28)	6.8 (15)	4.3 (14)	9.1 (10)	3.3 (15)	2.8 (16)
Other basic services											
Access to safe water	81.7 (27)	66.0 (41)	58.1 (19)	4.1 (27)	2.9 (41)	4.2 (19)	4.0 (12)	4.2 (12)	7.7 (8)	1.6 (14)	-3.5 (5)
Access to sanitation	73.9 (23)	57.6 (37)	41.6 (17)	2.6 (23)	4.4 (37)	6.7 (17)	3.2 (10)	2.7 (10)	14.2 (8)	3.5 (14)	-9.9 (3)

Sources: World Bank, World Development Indicators 1998 and 1999 database.

[1] Latest data available. Mostly refers to 1995–97. Except for life expectancy, which is in years, all the indicators refer to shares of the relevant population groups. See also Box 2.2.

[2] Nonprogram countries, shown for comparison, included Angola, The Bahamas, Bahrain, Belize, Bhutan, Botswana, Colombia, Cyprus, Eritrea, Fiji, Grenada, I.R. of Iran, Kuwait, Lebanon, Malaysia, Maldives, Malta, Myanmar, Namibia, Netherlands Antilles, Oman, Paraguay, Qatar, Seychelles, Solomon Islands, South Africa, St. Kitts and Nevis, St. Lucia, St. Vincent and the Grenadines, Swaziland, Syrian Arab Republic, Tonga, Turkmenistan, and United Arab Emirates.

[3] For infant mortality and under-5 mortality rates, number per thousand. The annual percent improvement in illiteracy, infant mortality, and under-5 mortality rates refers to a decline in these rates. An annual percent improvement of 3.4 in illiteracy, for example, means that illiteracy rates are falling by 3.4 percent per year.

[4] Gross enrollment rate is the ratio of total enrollment, regardless of age, to the population of the age group that corresponds to the level of education shown. If, for example because of grade repetition, students who fall outside the age bracket for primary or secondary education are nevertheless enrolled, the gross enrollment rate may exceed 100 percent.

[5] Contraceptive prevalence rate is the percentage of women who are practicing, or whose sexual partners are practicing, any form of contraception and is usually measured for women aged 15–49.

Figure 4.4. Benefit Incidence of Public Spending on Education and Health Care in Countries with IMF-Supported Programs, Early 1990s

(In percent of total spending; number of program countries in parentheses; latest year for which data are available)

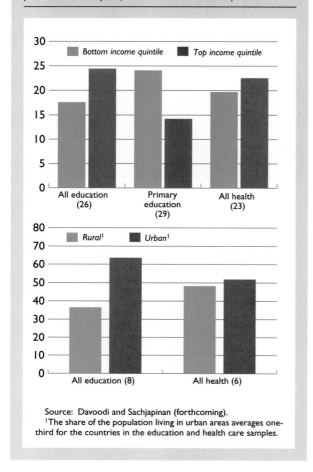

Source: Davoodi and Sachjapinan (forthcoming).
[1]The share of the population living in urban areas averages one-third for the countries in the education and health care samples.

education.[33] A similar urban bias emerges from limited data on health care spending for six countries.

Experience with Program Targets, Conditionality, and Monitoring in ESAF Countries

A review of 11 countries with ESAF arrangements illustrates a range of approaches and success with

public spending on education and health care.[34] It is difficult to establish any clear links between meeting benchmarks, performance criteria, and prior actions, on the one hand, and improved access to basic social services, on the other hand. Social indicators in ESAF countries, with the exception of the transition economies (Armenia, Georgia, and the Kyrgyz Republic), were generally poor at the outset of their programs. In nontransition countries, programs emphasized reorienting expenditures to raise spending on education and health care; in Bolivia, Lao People's Democratic Republic, and Uganda, deficit and/or overall expenditure levels were also programmed to rise as a share of GDP, in part to raise spending on education and health care. In the transition economies, where existing high and inefficient levels of education and health care spending tottered on a collapsing revenue base, programs emphasized quality and efficiency improvements.

In the nontransition countries the program objectives for education and health care spending were set in the context of longer-term goals drawn from the authorities' strategic plans for poverty reduction.[35]

- In several cases, the strategic plans were formal national government plans prepared in collaboration with the World Bank and other development partners (e.g., Bolivia, Côte d'Ivoire, Ghana, Malawi, and Uganda).

- In only a few countries were quantified long-term goals for social outcomes included explicitly in IMF-supported programs, for example, doubling the general literacy rate and increasing life expectancy to 57 years (Burkina Faso).

- For the HIPCs that reached the decision point (Bolivia, Burkina Faso, Côte d'Ivoire, Mozambique, and Uganda) and Ghana (1999), the use of quantitative goals for indicators was significantly expanded (Tables 4.2 and 4.3). In these cases, goals established for education and health care indicators were broadly in line with the OECD/UN/World Bank core set, with adjust-

---

[33]The rural population in Albania and Ghana, however, receives as much as 70 percent of the benefits from public spending on primary education. Furthermore, the incidence of education spending has improved over time in favor of the rural population in Malawi. See also Davoodi and Sachjapinan (forthcoming).

[34]The countries were selected to cover a range of social policy strategies and progress in implementing policies, with a view to identifying ways of strengthening the social content of IMF-supported programs. The ESAF arrangements reviewed cover the last five years, during which operational staff guidelines on public social spending were issued. The countries include five heavily indebted poor countries that have reached their decision point under the HIPC Initiative: Bolivia (with the three-year ESAF arrangements starting in 1994 and 1998); Burkina Faso (1998); Côte d'Ivoire (1998); Mozambique (1996); and Uganda (1997). Other countries included in the review are Armenia (1996); Georgia (1996); Kyrgyz Republic (1994 and 1998); Ghana (1995 and 1999); Lao People's Democratic Republic (1993); and Malawi (1995).

[35]In some cases, strategic plans specifically for the education and/or health care sectors were also formulated.

Table 4.2. Social Development Indicators, Selected ESAF Countries[1]

Indicators	HIPC Decision Point Countries				Other ESAF Country
	Bolivia	Burkina Faso	Mozambique	Uganda	Ghana
Education					
Admission and repetition rates for primary schools		X	X		
Gross/net enrollment ratios for primary and/or secondary schools	X	X		X	X
Primary school completion ratios	X			X	
Gender ratios (to increase ratio of girls to total pupils enrolled in primary schools)	X	X		X	
Book/pupil ratio		X			
Cumulative number of schools benefiting from participation in quality improvement programs	X				
Health					
Life expectancy					X
Fertility rate					X
Infant and maternal mortality rates					X
Child and/or pregnant woman vaccination rates	X	X		X	
DPT vaccination coverage	X		X		
Childhood malnutrition rate					X
Access to clean water				X	
Utilization rate of health centers		X			
Proportion of health posts staffed exclusively with untrained personnel			X		
Proportion of houses receiving measures against endemic diseases (e.g., chagas, malaria)	X				

[1]The countries included are a subset of the 11 ESAF countries for which the experience on program targets, conditionality, and monitoring was reviewed.

ments made for the authorities' specific objectives and local conditions.

- At the outset of the arrangements, the transition economies did not have overall poverty reduction plans, although for Armenia and Georgia poverty assessments had been completed by the World Bank at about the same time. In general, goals were cast in qualitative terms. For example, the long-term goals for spending on education and health care included a higher standard of living, development of human capital, and alleviation of poverty (Bolivia); better provision of social services by enhancing the efficiency of social expenditures (Georgia); improving basic education and health care and human resources (Ghana); and providing adequate funding for human development and improving living standards (Lao People's Democratic Republic).

All of the programs reviewed included measures to improve fiscal governance. In general, these reforms addressed broad expenditure management issues and covered the setting of budgetary spending allocations and priorities, expenditure controls, and reporting, as well as transparency.[36] In Mozambique, reforms included the publication of budget plans and outcomes.

Programs often focused on improving cost-effectiveness and spending composition.

- To this end, programs often included measures to reduce the cost of delivery of social services (e.g., reducing excessive numbers of teachers) and to improve the quality of spending (e.g., improving the school curriculum and introducing second shifts in schools to overcome capacity constraints on the feasible number of hours of teaching).

- Program targets for public spending sought to reorient expenditure composition toward education and health care and, in particular, protect such spending during fiscal adjustment. Most of the

---

[36]In the Kyrgyz Republic (1998) and Burkina Faso (1996), some of the reforms were directly targeted at social spending.

Table 4.3.   Monitoring Arrangements, Selected ESAF Countries[1]

Ghana
A broad-based Technical Committee on Poverty comprising officials from various ministries and government departments, donors, and NGOs was established in 1997 and meets regularly. The committee collects and disseminates information on poverty reduction programs. As part of this Continuous Poverty Monitoring System, a pilot survey has been undertaken to provide a systematic and frequent update on key poverty indicators. Also, donor committees meet frequently on health and education issues to coordinate, exchange information, and monitor programs.

Malawi
A governmental poverty and social policy monitoring unit was established in 1995 to monitor core social indicators to be presented to donors and at Consultative Group meetings.

Uganda
A poverty monitoring unit including education, finance, and health ministry officials was established in 1998 and made responsible for collecting poverty and social sector information at the local level. Health districts collect quarterly data on health-related indicators and report them to the sector monitoring unit. Expenditure tracking studies were undertaken to identify obstacles that prevented budgeted expenditures from reaching their intended use.

[1]The countries included are a subset of the 11 ESAF countries for which the experience on program targets, conditionality, and monitoring was reviewed.

the earlier ESAF-supported programs did not include quantitative budget targets for education and health care spending at their outset, but these were introduced at a later stage (Table 4.4). This in part reflected the introduction in 1997 of staff operational guidelines on social spending. All of the programs of the heavily indebted poor countries that had reached their decision points under the HIPC Initiative have included quantitative targets. In the transition economies, part of the strategy for increasing access to education and health care services has been to involve the private sector.

The scope of spending targets that could be monitored was constrained. The constraints included a lack of data on the intrasectoral allocation of education and health care spending, incomplete coverage of these sectors, and lags in the availability of data. Quantitative spending targets and benchmarks singled out education and health care spending as priorities to be protected from cuts

(Bolivia, Kyrgyz Republic, Malawi, and Uganda), or aimed at redirecting public spending in favor of education and health care (Ghana and Malawi) (see Table 4.4). Because the link between expenditure on education and health care and final outcomes is complex and uncertain, programs monitored actual spending and developments in intermediate social indicators such as the hiring or firing of teachers and consolidation of schools (Armenia), increasing water supply and number of classrooms created (Côte d'Ivoire), reducing stays in hospitals (the Kyrgyz Republic), and increasing the share of textbooks in the budget (Malawi). Monitoring was also undertaken with a view to assessing the impact of policies on the provision of social services. Program documents also have included qualitative assessments of progress.

A number of innovations have strengthened monitoring.

* The introduction of explicit targets has contributed to improved monitoring of developments. The staff reports on programs of the HIPCs that had reached the decision point (Bolivia, Burkina Faso, Côte d'Ivoire, Mozambique, and Uganda) have systematically covered developments relating to spending targets and social outcomes. In the other countries, the onset of improved monitoring also has reflected the issuance of the staff guidelines on social spending. But significant weaknesses remain in the quality of reporting in some countries. For instance, definitions of targeted spending as set out in the initial request for the ESAF arrangement and those that were subsequently monitored have sometimes been different. As noted earlier, information on actual spending was typically available only with a considerable time lag, which meant that targets had to be based on partial estimates for the preceding year(s). As a result, a clear picture of spending developments and their impact on social indicators emerged only after the passage of several annual programs.

* In more recent ESAF-supported programs, formulating a clear framework in program documents that integrated social spending targets with a time path of specified indicators and outcomes improved the focus and monitoring of social policy. Such frameworks were used in the case of HIPCs that had reached the decision point and in Ghana's program (1999). In these cases, the authorities explicitly noted their commitment to education and health care output targets in the Memorandum of Economic Policies (MEP), reinforcing the emphasis given to social issues in the Policy Frame-

Table 4.4. Public Education and Health Care Spending Targets, Selected ESAF Countries[1]

Country[2]	Quantified Expenditure Target	Definition	Monitoring[3]	Comment
Transition Economies				
Armenia (1996)	Yes	Current health and education expenditures in percent of GDP.	Yes	Quantitative target specified and monitored from the second annual arrangement.
Georgia (1996)	Yes	Social expenditures in percent of GDP (1996).	Yes	Quantitative targets specified in the reports but definitions differ across reports. Reports include mostly qualitative discussion of social expenditure developments, but without reference to previously specified targets.
		Budgetary appropriations for health and education (from 1997).		
Kyrgyz Republic (1994)	No	—	—	
Kyrgyz Republic (1998)[4]	Yes	Health and education expenditures in percent of GDP and total spending.	Yes	—
HIPC at Decision Point				
Bolivia (1995)	Yes	Health and education expenditures in percent of GDP.	Yes	Quantitative target specified and monitored from the third annual arrangement.
Bolivia (1999)	Yes	Health and education expenditures in percent of GDP.	Yes	—
Burkina Faso (1996)	Yes	Health and primary education expenditures in percent of GDP.	Yes	—
Côte d'Ivoire (1998)	Yes	Health and education expenditures in percent of GDP.	Yes	—
Mozambique (1996)	Yes	Current expenditures on health and education in percent of GDP.	Yes	Quantitative target specified and monitored from the second annual arrangement.
Uganda (1997)	Yes	Health and education expenditures in percent of GDP.	Yes	—
Other ESAF Countries				
Ghana (1995)	Yes	Health and education expenditures, excluding foreign financed capital expenditures, in percent of GDP.	Yes	Target specified and monitored from the second annual arrangement.
Ghana (1999)	Yes	Health and education expenditures, excluding foreign financed capital expenditures, in percent of GDP.	Yet to be reviewed	—
Lao People's Democratic Republic (1993)	No	—	—	—
Malawi (1995)	Yes	Current expenditures on health and education in percent of GDP.	Yes	Quantitative target specified and monitored from the third annual arrangement. Definition of targets differs across reports. Qualitative discussion of social expenditure and outcome developments, including with reference to previously specified quantitative target.

Source: IMF staff reports.

[1]A program is defined to have a quantitative target when either the staff report, MEP, and/or PFP provides a projection for the category of public spending. This is a broader coverage than used in Box 4.2, which is restricted to MEPs and PFPs.

[2]Year of program approval in parentheses.

[3]Defined as a reference to and/or a discussion of the developments with respect to the quantitative target specified in the request for the ESAF arrangement or subsequent annual arrangements.

[4]Program has performance criteria set in nominal terms as a floor on expenditures on health and education.

work Papers (PFP). The advantages of a well-defined framework also carried through to more focused, comprehensive, and forward-looking assessments of education and health care sector developments. In other countries, improved monitoring of education and health care spending is evident in programs approved after 1997, following the introduction of the staff guidelines on social spending, and program documents provide more specific information on related developments and report spending on education and health care at a disaggregated level.

• In the HIPC decision point countries and Ghana, information to monitor social developments was drawn from a wider variety of sources, including bilateral donors (Burkina Faso and Ghana). These arrangements also made effective use of information from internal reviews conducted at the local government and community levels. Also, in several countries, poverty monitoring teams and units were set up (examples are given in Table 4.3).

In specifying public spending targets and policy measures and in monitoring, IMF staff collaborated with the World Bank and regional development banks. The World Bank provided policy analyses for many countries. Except for Burkina Faso and Georgia, however, comprehensive World Bank Public Expenditure Reviews were not available at the time of the initial request for an ESAF arrangement to guide budget policy. Thus, it was not always possible to ensure that budget allocations for education and health care were in line with an appropriate overall composition of expenditures. Expenditure reviews have since been undertaken or are scheduled to commence in 1999 in all 11 countries.

Conditionality[37] was attached to public spending targets and to key reforms for which timely implementation was essential to the success of the program.

• Conditionality was used sparingly, and primarily took the form of benchmarks[38] (Table 4.5). Performance criteria and prior actions have rarely been used. For the most part, conditionality was applied to minimum levels of budget spending with a view to protecting spending on education and health care from the pressure of overall spending restraint, in parallel with World Bank programs to improve the quality of social sector spending (Georgia and the Kyrgyz Republic), or to ensure that additional resources were not diverted to other uses (Uganda).

• Conditionality was used to encourage the timely completion of sector and national poverty reduction strategies and action plans, which were prerequisites for establishing a clear operational strategy for improving access to social services over the medium term. In Côte d'Ivoire a prior action on adopting an antipoverty national plan was introduced to provide stronger evidence of the authorities' commitment to strengthening spending on education and health care, an area in which there had been slippage and an unmet benchmark in the previous ESAF arrangement. Establishing performance criteria on education and health care spending in the Kyrgyz Republic and Uganda programs was combined with measures to ensure the quality of such spending.

---

[37]Policy measures that members intend to follow as a condition for the use of IMF financial resources.

[38]The link between disbursements of financial assistance and adherence to benchmarks is less strict than for performance criteria and prior actions.

Table 4.5. Social Policy Conditionality (Prior Actions, Performance Criteria, and Benchmarks), Selected ESAF Countries[1]

Country	ESAF Arrangement[2]	Policy Measure	Conditionality	Type of Observance
Armenia	ESAF. 3 (1998)	Develop and approve a three-year strategic plan for the health sector by end-September 1999.	Benchmark	Review pending
Côte d'Ivoire	ESAF. 1 (1998)	Adopt a national plan to fight poverty.	Prior action	Met
Georgia	ESAF. 1 (1996)	Reduce number of budgetary positions, primarily in education, by 10,000 by September 1996.	Benchmark	Met
	ESAF. 2 (1997)	Minimum amount of health expenditures of the republican government cumulative from January 1, 1997.	Benchmark	Not met
	ESAF. 3 (1998)	Minimum amount of health expenditures of the republican government.	Benchmark	Not met
Ghana	ESAF. 2 (1995)	Complete medium-term expenditure framework (MTEF) for priority sectors of education, health, and roads.	Performance criteria	Met
Kyrgyz Republic	ESAF. 1 (1998)	Cumulative floor on budgetary expenditures separately on health and education beginning April 1998.[3]	Performance criteria	Waived[4]
Mozambique	ESAF. 3 (1998)	Complete National Poverty Assessment and Poverty Action Plan by end-1998.	Benchmark	Met
Uganda	ESAF. 1 (1997)	Minimum amount of nonwage expenditures on priority program areas in health and education.	Benchmark	Met
	ESAF. 2 (1998)	Minimum amount of nonwage expenditures on priority program areas including universal primary education component of domestic development expenditures.	Performance criteria	Met

Source: IMF staff reports.

[1]Social policy conditionalities were used in only 7 of the 11 ESAF countries.

[2]Year of program approval shown in parentheses; suffix indicates the program year (1 to 3).

[3]Program targets are set in terms of expenditures as a percent of GDP.

[4]Prior actions on the level of spending in the quarter following the test date were set as conditions for completing the midterm review, of which that on health was met. In addition, measures to strengthen overall expenditure management were to be introduced and the authorities undertook to ensure that spending on education and health care would be kept at least constant in real terms throughout 1999.

V Collaboration with the World Bank and Other International Agencies

The IMF is concerned with the social dimensions of its economic policy advice. The analysis and policy advice on social issues, however, are to a large extent outside the principal areas of IMF expertise. Between the Bretton Woods institutions, the primary responsibility for social policies lies with the World Bank, and IMF staff relies upon the World Bank in this area. Other international institutions, such as regional development banks and UN agencies (e.g., International Labor Organization, United Nations Development Program, and World Health Organization), the donor community, NGOs, and civil society, on a country-by-country basis, also can provide valuable inputs.

World Bank and IMF staffs have well-established procedures for collaboration, including on social sector issues, in support of members' efforts to achieve sustainable growth and poverty reduction.[39] On social sector issues, IMF staff looks to the World Bank for inputs on social sector policy goals, analysis, reforms, and their budgetary cost, as well as data on social indicators. An iterative interaction between the staffs of the IMF and the World Bank ensures the consistency of the overall macroeconomic framework, including notably the fiscal envelope, with sustainable, cost-effective social policies and strategies for poverty reduction.

Frequent interaction between the staffs of the World Bank and the IMF on social issues takes place through several channels.

- In addition to exchanges at headquarters, including through the review process, IMF missions to program countries have usually involved parallel World Bank missions or the participation of World Bank staff (and vice versa), as well as in-field consultations with resident representatives. In ESAF countries, overlapping missions are the norm.
- In ESAF-supported programs, the PFP includes a separate section on poverty and social sector issues.

- Reflecting the joint nature of the HIPC Initiative and its specific emphasis on achieving social improvements and development, collaboration is intensive in HIPCs, particularly as they approach their decision points under the Initiative.
- In the fall of 1998, a pilot program for enhanced World Bank–IMF collaboration in low-income (ESAF/IDA) countries was launched in six countries (Cameroon, Ethiopia, Nicaragua, Tajikistan, Vietnam, and Zimbabwe). The pilot includes a specific focus on social sector issues; in particular, it is envisaged that the World Bank would not only identify measures to mitigate adverse effects on the poor and vulnerable, but also assess the social impact of program design more broadly, ex ante and ex post.
- Periodically, joint institution-wide, forward-looking reviews of work plans and priorities in public sector work are carried out. These reviews aim, among other things, to coordinate IMF and World Bank public sector work and to ensure the timely availability of public expenditure analyses.
- At the general policy level, the IMF's Fiscal Affairs Department and its World Bank counterparts in the Poverty Reduction and Economic Management and Human Development Networks have recently initiated regular senior-level meetings to coordinate work programs and to help resolve collaboration issues that may arise.

The importance of social sector issues for the IMF has led to a strengthening of collaboration with the UN system and regional development banks. For example, in the area of labor market and related social policy reform, guidelines were issued in 1996 to IMF staff on collaboration with the International Labor Organization (ILO) that provide for more systematic contacts between staff at the country level, especially through resident representatives. Also, pilot countries were selected for enhanced IMF-ILO collaboration, and interaction on general policy issues has been increased, most recently in the context

---

[39]Collaboration between the World Bank and IMF has been periodically reviewed and staff guidance notes on collaboration in certain policy areas have been issued.

of the Asian crisis.[40] In late 1998, the World Health Organization (WHO) and the IMF strengthened collaboration on health-related issues in low-income countries.

World Bank–IMF collaboration in the social area, however, has not always been seamless. In part, this reflects a mismatch between the timetables adopted for World Bank and IMF work programs and the operational methods of IMF- and World Bank-supported programs, which, in some respects, are not well-attuned to each other since IMF-supported programs are typically formulated under relatively tight deadlines, often demanded by a crisis situation.

- The pressing country requirements can, unfortunately, cut across the grain of the longer time frame of preparatory work, including a broad participatory approach for social policy formulation. This highlights the importance of an ex ante dialogue and ongoing policy analysis and recommendations in the social policy area.

- Sufficient time is also not always available to collect information to develop well-targeted social sector reforms.

- On occasion, World Bank input has not been available within the time frame required by the countries' circumstances, and the IMF staff and the country authorities have devised policies as best they could. In such cases, the focus has tended to be on mitigating the adverse impact on vulnerable groups through specific social protection mechanisms, rather than in terms of program design based on ex ante social assessments.

From an IMF perspective, more World Bank involvement, including in monitoring and following up on social sector issues, would be desirable, particularly for ESAF countries. The World Bank has shifted away from comprehensive Public Expenditure Reviews (PERs) toward a sequence of more in-depth sector-specific expenditure reviews, which are useful in their own right, but do not provide a comprehensive analysis of budget priorities. The World Bank staff understandably focuses their work programs on the Country Assistance Strategies (CASs) and their own lending operations. Thus, the PFP is not regarded as a priority in the work agenda of World Bank staff. It is no longer discussed by the World Bank's Executive Board and is generally not directly relevant to World Bank's operations, which contrasts with the role of the Policy Framework

Paper (PFP) at the IMF. This difference has created gaps in needed inputs for ESAF-supported and other programs and has, in some cases, led IMF staff to work with the authorities to fill the gap through IMF technical assistance.

The most recent internal assessment of the World Bank's support of poverty reduction found that, relative to past benchmarks, performance has been good (World Bank, 1999). At the same time, it raised many of the same concerns noted above.[41] As a result, mechanisms for more active monitoring of developments in these areas are being implemented. Various World Bank initiatives should contribute to a better and more systematic integration of social sector issues in World Bank lending operations and hence in IMF-supported programs:

- developing the Comprehensive Development Framework (CDF), which includes countries' social sector objectives and policies;

- strengthening the poverty focus in Country Assistance Strategies;

- preparing social and structural policy reviews;

- improving the delivery of Public Expenditure Reviews and their synchronization with countries' budget processes;

- implementing the joint ESAF/IDA pilot scheme; and

- developing and implementing the Principles and Good Practices in Social Policy.

World Bank–IMF collaboration in the poverty reduction and social policy area could be strengthened by the formulation, together with the authorities, of a Poverty Reduction Strategy Paper (PRSP) through a participatory process. The PRSP would aim at ensuring the consistency between a country's macroeconomic, structural, and social policies, and the goals of poverty reduction and social development. It would

- be owned by the government and endorsed by the Boards of the World Bank and the IMF as a basis for the institutions' operations;

- include a macroeconomic framework and structural and social policies consistent with the poverty reduction and social goals;

---

[40]IMF senior staff have participated in the high-level tripartite ILO meetings in Bangkok in 1997, 1998, and 1999, and, in May 1998, the IMF organized a seminar with the ILO to improve the staff's understanding of core labor standards and the ILO's role in setting and monitoring these standards.

[41]The World Bank report underscored three points: (i) only somewhat more than half of the Country Assistance Strategies prepared in FY1998 were judged fully satisfactory in their integration of poverty issues into the framing of a forward-looking strategy; (ii) progress in completing poverty assessments has at times been slow, reflecting a greater use of participatory and consultative methods, staff resource constraints, and the degree of domestic political commitment; and (iii) much less progress has been made in evaluating the impact of specific interventions (only 13 percent of Country Assistance Strategies include monitorable poverty benchmarks that were time-bound and output- or outcome-oriented).

- set out technical assistance needs and expected providers; and
- identify overall external financing needs.

When all these elements are available in the PRSP, it could replace the Policy Framework Paper

and provide a framework for World Bank and IMF lending operations for the country.[42] While the PRSP might be prepared every three years, there would be annual updates.

---

[42]A more detailed description of the proposed process and the PRSP is provided in the Bank-IMF paper, "HIPC Initiative—

Strengthening the Link Between Debt Relief and Poverty Reduction," which is available on the Internet at http://www.imf.org/external/np/pdr/prsp/status.htm.

VI Afterword: The Poverty Reduction and Growth Facility

Following the Executive Board's consideration of this and other papers, important changes were made to the ESAF to give the goal of poverty reduction greater prominence and improve its effectiveness as a policy instrument to favor growth and reduce poverty.

The key change is that the complementarity of macroeconomic, structural, and social policies will be given greater recognition. These policies will be articulated in a Poverty Reduction Strategy Paper (PRSP), which will integrate these policies in a mutually reinforcing manner. Many of the recommendations for strengthening the design and implementation of social policies, particularly in efficiency and targeting of public spending, will feed into the PRSP. Importantly, the PRSP prepared in collaboration with the IMF and World Bank will be nationally owned: the preparation will be government-led based on an open consultative process, including with civil society. The PRSP will also serve as the vehicle for strengthened IMF–World Bank collaboration. Reflecting these changes, the ESAF was renamed the Poverty Reduction and Growth Facility in November 1999.

Appendix   IMF Executive Board Discussion

Directors considered that the IMF's primary role is to promote macroeconomic stability and structural reforms necessary for achieving sustainable and rapid growth. They underscored the crucial importance of economic growth for poverty alleviation, but also recognized that the IMF must be sensitive to the social implications of its policy advice. In particular, Directors noted that IMF-supported programs have sought to help members address the potential adverse impact on vulnerable groups of their adjustment and reform efforts as well as of exogenous shocks, and that such efforts in turn can make a vital contribution toward sustaining economic reforms and protecting living standards. They also observed that sound macroeconomic policies, coupled with effective social and infrastructure spending, foster faster long-term growth. In light of these considerations, Directors observed that social safety nets and appropriately targeted productive public spending, particularly in the social area, can provide critical support for the success of members' adjustment and reform programs.

Broader requirements for improving living standards were also discussed, including promoting faster growth and employment creation and better integrating poorer countries into the international economic system. In addition, Directors suggested that the international community should work to improve these countries' access to industrial country markets, as well as to halt the excessive flow of weapons to developing countries. Directors stressed the importance of good governance, transparency, and accountability for ensuring the effective use of public resources.

Directors discussed the role of the IMF with regard to social policies. Recognizing the need for mutually reinforcing macroeconomic and social policies, they underscored the importance of more closely integrating, with the help of the World Bank, social issues and poverty concerns into IMF-supported programs. Directors agreed that greater attention to social issues was necessary in the context of low-income countries, including HIPCs, where structural reforms are particularly critical. With regard to other countries, a variety of views was expressed on the degree and modalities of IMF involvement in social issues. Some speakers attached importance to these issues in countries other than low-income countries, pointing to the recent experience in the Asian crisis countries and elsewhere. However, a number of Directors, while concurring that IMF-supported programs should encompass members' social policies and poverty reduction efforts, cautioned nevertheless that the IMF should not allow its primary mandate to be diluted. They viewed the World Bank as taking the leading role in developing adequate social safety nets and effective social policies, and the IMF as contributing to poverty reduction mainly through its support of economic policies that provide a conducive environment for sustained growth.

All Directors emphasized that, as regards social issues, the World Bank and other relevant international organizations have the primary mandate and expertise. In this connection, they noted, for example, that the relationship between public social spending, growth, and poverty is complex, and that it is therefore critical to ensure that spending is used productively. Several Directors cautioned that the IMF did not have the panoply of expertise needed to assess the quality of social spending and related issues. Directors, therefore, underscored that the social components of countries' IMF-supported programs should draw, to the fullest extent possible, on the work of the World Bank and other relevant institutions. Some Directors were of the view that when timely inputs from these institutions on essential social components of IMF-supported programs were not available, IMF staff would necessarily have to provide policy advice to the extent feasible. Many other Directors were skeptical about such IMF involvement, particularly if it were to require additional staff expertise. All Directors suggested that, to facilitate such cooperation, these institutions should be encouraged to provide more timely input. Over-

---

Note: Summing up provided by the Chairman of the Executive Board after the discussion on September 19,1999, of the paper on social issues and policies in IMF-supported programs.

all, Directors agreed that more intensive cooperation between the IMF and the Bank is essential, proceeding along the lines of these institutions' respective responsibilities and comparative advantages, and thus avoiding duplication of efforts. They welcomed therefore the recent enhanced IMF-Bank cooperation, pointing to the Enhanced Structural Adjustment Facility/International Development Association (ESAF/IDA) pilot program and the preparation of the reports for this discussion.

Turning to specific issues in the area of social policies, Directors noted the scope for further improving the quality and implementation of social safety nets, through comprehensive ex ante analyses and monitoring, relying on the expertise of the World Bank and other organizations. Several Directors recommended that the staff should assess, in the course of surveillance, the adequacy of social policy instruments, the performance of social safety nets, and the potential social ramifications of macroeconomic and financial policies. Many others, however, cautioned that this should not detract from the appropriate focus of Article IV surveillance. We will have to come back to this matter on the occasion of the biennial review of surveillance.

Spending on education and health care has increased in real per capita terms and in relation to GDP in most countries with IMF-supported programs during the past decade. While this has been accompanied by an improvement in a broad range of social indicators, Directors noted the diversity in outcomes caused by the differences in the effectiveness of social spending. Although some cautioned that too much emphasis on the absolute amount of social spending could send the wrong message, Directors more generally stressed the importance of efficient and well-targeted spending for ensuring that gains in social indicators are commensurate with spending increases. Further improvements in these areas could be achieved, inter alia, by strengthening a country's budget formulation and implementation capacity.

The establishment of national quantitative targets for poverty reduction—consistent with the International Development Goals for 2015 to which countries have subscribed—could also prove beneficial, especially if the higher targeted spending is used productively. Directors suggested that, in setting targets, spending needs in priority areas for poverty reduction other than health, education, and social safety nets—such as basic sanitation, rural roads, and access to clean water—should also be taken into account; such priority spending may contribute as much or more to poverty reduction. Some Directors thought that core labor standards had a valuable contribution to make to the achievement of these targets, while other Directors were concerned that this issue is outside the IMF's main areas of responsibility. We will come back to this issue after further consultations with the World Bank and the ILO.

Directors considered that in countries where social spending is so low as to be a critical area of weakness, structural benchmarks could continue to be used selectively to protect social spending and to promote key institutional reforms. While many Directors thought that such benchmarks should only be used in ESAF-supported programs, some other Directors saw the value in applying performance indicators (performance criteria and structural benchmarks) to a broader range of IMF-supported programs. In establishing such structural benchmarks, IMF staff will rely on inputs from the World Bank and others to ensure, inter alia, the targeting and quality of spending.

Directors noted with concern the widespread poor quality of data on social spending, social indicators, and social protection arrangements, which inhibited the design and implementation of effective social programs. They saw an urgent need for country authorities to identify weaknesses in data and data collection, and to make data improvements in collaboration with the World Bank, other international agencies, and civil society.

References

Abed, George, and others, 1998, *Fiscal Reforms in Low-Income Countries: Experience Under IMF-Supported Programs*, IMF Occasional Paper No. 160 (Washington: International Monetary Fund).

Anand, Sudhir, and Martin Ravallion, 1993, "Human Development in Poor Countries: On the Role of Private Incomes and Public Services," *Journal of Economic Perspectives,* Vol. 7 (Winter), No. 1, pp. 133–50.

Aninat, Eduardo, Andreas Bauer, and Kevin Cowan, 1999, "Addressing Equity Issues in Policymaking: Lessons from the Chilean Experience," in *Economic Policy and Equity,* ed. by Vito Tanzi, Ke-young Chu, and Sanjeev Gupta (Washington: International Monetary Fund).

Barro, Robert, 1995, "Inflation and Economic Growth," *Bank of England Quarterly Bulletin,* Vol. 35 (May), pp. 166–76.

Bidani, Benu, and Martin Ravallion, 1997, "Decomposing Social Indicators Using Distributional Data," *Journal of Econometrics,* Vol. 77 (March), No. 1, pp. 125–93.

Bredenkamp, Hugh, and Susan Schadler, 1999, *Economic Adjustment and Reform in Low-Income Countries* (Washington: International Monetary Fund).

Bruno, Michael, and William Easterly, 1995, "Inflation Crises and Long-Run Growth," NBER Working Paper No. 5209 (Cambridge, Massachusetts: National Bureau of Economic Research).

Bulír, Aleš, 1998, "Income Inequality: Does Inflation Matter?" IMF Working Paper 98/7 (Washington: International Monetary Fund).

———, and Anne-Marie Gulde, 1995, "Inflation and Income Distribution: Further Evidence on Empirical Links," IMF Working Paper 95/86 (Washington: International Monetary Fund).

Chu, Ke-young, and Sanjeev Gupta, eds., 1998, *Social Safety Nets: Issues and Recent Experiences* (Washington: International Monetary Fund).

Cox, Donald, Zekeriya Eser, and Emmanuel Jimenez, 1997, "Family Safety Nets During Economic Transition," in *Poverty in Russia: Public Policy and Private Responses,* ed. by Jeni Klugman (Washington: Economic Development Institute of the World Bank).

Cox, Donald, Wlodek Okrasa, and Emmanuel Jimenez, 1997, "Family Safety Nets and Economic Transition: A Study of Households in Poland," *Review of Income and Wealth,* Vol. 43 (June), No. 2, pp. 191–209.

Davoodi, Hamid R., and Sawitree Sachjapinan, forthcoming, "How Useful Are Benefit Incidence Studies?" IMF Working Paper (Washington: International Monetary Fund).

Demery, Lionel, and Lyn Squire, 1996, "Macroeconomic Adjustment and Poverty in Africa: An Emerging Picture," *The World Bank Research Observer,* Vol. 11 (February), No. 1, pp. 39–60.

Easterly, William, and Sergio Rebelo, 1993, "Fiscal Policy and Economic Growth: An Empirical Investigation," NBER Working Paper No. 4499 (Cambridge, Massachusetts: National Bureau of Economic Research).

Ferreira, Francisco, Giovanna Prennushi, and Martin Ravallion, 1999, "Protecting the Poor from Macroeconomic Shocks: An Agenda for Action in a Crisis and Beyond," Policy Research Working Paper No. 2160 (Washington: World Bank).

Filmer, Deon, Jeffrey Hammer, and Lant Pritchett, 1998, "Health Policy in Poor Countries: Weak Links in the Chain," Policy Research Working Paper No. 1874 (Washington: World Bank).

Fischer, Stanley, 1991, "Growth, Macroeconomics, and Development," NBER Working Paper No. 3702 (Cambridge, Massachusetts: National Bureau of Economic Research).

Frankenberg, Elizabeth, Duncan Thomas, and Kathleen Beegle, 1999, "The Real Costs of Indonesia's Economic Crisis: Preliminary Findings from the Indonesia Family Life Surveys," Labor and Population Program Working Paper 99-04 (Santa Monica: RAND).

Ghosh, Atish, and Steven Phillips, 1998, "Warning: Inflation May Be Harmful to Your Growth," *Staff Papers,* International Monetary Fund, Vol. 45 (December), pp. 672–710.

Goldsbrough, David, and others, 1996, *Reinvigorating Growth in Developing Countries: Lessons from Adjustment Policies in Eight Economies,* IMF Occasional Paper No. 139 (Washington: International Monetary Fund).

Guitián, Manuel, 1998, "Monetary Policy: Equity Issues in IMF Policy Advice," in *Income Distribution and High-Quality Growth,* ed. by Vito Tanzi and Ke-young Chu (Cambridge, Massachusetts: MIT Press).

Gupta, Sanjeev, 1998, "Economic Transition and Social Protection: Issues and Agenda for Reform," IMF Paper on Policy Analysis and Assessment 98/14 (Washington: International Monetary Fund).

———, Marijn Verhoeven, and Keiko Honjo, 1997, "The Efficiency of Government Expenditures: Experiences from Africa," IMF Working Paper 97/153 (Washington: International Monetary Fund).

Gupta, Sanjeev, and others, 1998, *The IMF and the Poor*, IMF Pamphlet Series, No. 52 (Washington: International Monetary Fund).

Gupta, Sanjeev, Marijn Verhoeven, and Erwin Tiongson, 1999, "Does Higher Government Spending Buy Better Results in Education and Health Care?" IMF Working Paper 99/21 (Washington: International Monetary Fund).

Gupta, Sanjeev, Marijn Verhoeven, Gustavo Yamada, and Erwin Tiongson, 1999, "Education and Health Spending Continues Rise in Countries with IMF-Supported Programs," *IMF Survey* (March 8), pp. 79–80.

Harberger, Arnold C., 1998, "Monetary and Fiscal Policy for Equitable Economic Growth," in *Income Distribution and High-Quality Growth*, ed. by Vito Tanzi and Ke-young Chu (Cambridge, Massachusetts: MIT Press).

Iglesias, Enrique V., 1999, "Equity Issues in Latin America," in *Economic Policy and Equity*, ed. by Vito Tanzi, Ke-young Chu, and Sanjeev Gupta (Washington: International Monetary Fund).

International Monetary Fund, 1986, *Fund-Supported Programs, Fiscal Policy, and Income Distribution*, IMF Occasional Paper No. 46 (Washington: International Monetary Fund).

———, 1995, *Social Dimensions of the IMF's Policy Dialogue*, prepared by the Staff of the International Monetary Fund, IMF Pamphlet Series, No. 47 (Washington: International Monetary Fund).

———, 1996, "Partnership for Sustainable Global Growth," an Interim Committee Declaration, *IMF Survey*, October 14, p. 327.

———, 1997, *The ESAF at Ten Years: Economic Adjustment and Reform in Low-Income Countries*, IMF Occasional Paper No. 156 (Washington: International Monetary Fund).

Levine, Ross, and Sara Zervos, 1993, "Looking at the Facts: What We Know About Policy and Growth from Cross-Country Analysis," Policy Research Working Paper No. 1115 (Washington: World Bank).

Mauro, Paulo, 1998, "Corruption and the Composition of Government Expenditure," *Journal of Public Economics*, Vol. 69 (August), No. 2, pp. 263–79.

Milanovic, Branko, 1994, "Determinants of Cross-Country Income Inequality: An 'Augmented' Kuznets'

Hypothesis," Policy Research Working Paper No. 1246 (Washington: World Bank).

Mingat, Alain, and Jee-Peng Tan, 1998, "The Mechanics of Progress in Education: Evidence from Cross-Country Data," Policy Research Working Paper No. 2015 (Washington: World Bank).

Sahn, David E., Paul A. Dorosh, and Stephen D. Younger, 1997, *Structural Adjustment Reconsidered: Economic Policy and Poverty in Africa* (New York: Cambridge University Press).

Sarel, Michael, 1996, "Nonlinear Effects of Inflation on Economic Growth," *Staff Papers*, International Monetary Fund, Vol. 43 (March), No. 4, pp. 199–215.

———, 1997, "How Macroeconomic Factors Affect Income Distribution: The Cross-Country Evidence," IMF Working Paper 97/152 (Washington: International Monetary Fund).

Sen, Amartya, 1999, "Economic Policy and Equity: An Overview," in *Economic Policy and Equity*, ed. by Vito Tanzi, Ke-young Chu, and Sanjeev Gupta (Washington: International Monetary Fund).

Subbarao, K., and others, 1997, *Safety Net Programs and Poverty Reduction: Lessons from Cross-Country Experience* (Washington: World Bank).

Tanzi, Vito, 1998, "Corruption Around the World: Causes, Consequences, Scope, and Cures," *Staff Papers*, International Monetary Fund, Vol. 45 (December), pp. 559–94.

——— and Ke-young Chu, eds., 1998, *Income Distribution and High-Quality Growth* (Cambridge, Massachusetts: MIT Press).

——— and Sanjeev Gupta, eds., 1999, *Economic Policy and Equity* (Washington: International Monetary Fund).

Ter-Minassian, Teresa, ed., 1997, *Fiscal Federalism in Theory and Practice* (Washington: International Monetary Fund).

World Bank, 1993, *World Development Report 1993: Investing in Health* (Washington: World Bank).

———, 1995, *Priorities and Strategies for Education: A World Bank Review* (Washington: World Bank).

———, 1996, *Social Dimensions of Adjustment: World Bank Experience, 1980–93* (Washington: World Bank).

———, 1999, *Poverty Reduction and the World Bank: Progress in Fiscal 1998* (Washington: World Bank).

Glossary

Benchmarks. In the context of IMF-supported programs, a point of reference against which program implementation is monitored. Benchmarks are not necessarily quantitative and frequently relate to structural variables and policies.

Comprehensive Development Framework (CDF). A holistic approach to development formulated by the World Bank and implemented on a pilot basis since early 1999. The CDF highlights the interdependence of all elements of development—social, structural, human, governance, environmental, economic, and financial—and stresses ownership by the country and partnership with government, civil society, assistance agencies, and the private sector.

Conditionality. Economic policies that members intend to follow as a condition for the use of IMF resources. These are often expressed as performance criteria (e.g., monetary and budgetary targets) or benchmarks, and are intended to ensure that the use of IMF credit is temporary and consistent with the objectives of adjustment programs designed to correct a member's macroeconomic and structural imbalances, and promote stronger growth and external payments viability.

Country Assistance Strategy (CAS). The central vehicle for World Bank Executive Board review of its assistance strategy for the International Development Association (IDA) and its borrowers. The CAS document describes the strategy based on an assessment of priorities in the country and indicates the level and composition of assistance to be provided based on the strategy and the country's portfolio performance.

Enhanced Structural Adjustment Facility (ESAF). This facility, established by the Executive Board in 1987 and extended and enlarged in February 1994, was the principal means by which the IMF provided financial support, in the form of highly concessional loans, to low-income member countries facing protracted balance of payments problems and loans and grants under the HIPC Initiative. In late 1999, the ESAF was succeeded by the Poverty Reduction and Growth Facility (PRGF).

ESAF/IDA Pilot Project. Program for enhanced World Bank–IMF collaboration in low-income (ESAF/IDA) countries, including a specific focus on social sector issues in six countries—Cameroon, Ethiopia, Nicaragua, Tajikistan, Vietnam, and Zimbabwe.

Heavily Indebted Poor Countries (HIPC) Initiative. Initiative designed to provide exceptional assistance to heavily indebted poor countries following sound economic policies to help them reduce their external debt burden to sustainable levels. In the second half of 1999, the Initiative was strengthened to provide deeper and faster debt relief through the Enhanced HIPC Initiative.

Memorandum of Economic Policies (MEP). Document prepared by a member country describing the policies that it intends to implement in the context of its request for financial support from the IMF.

Performance Criteria. Macroeconomic indicators such as monetary and budgetary targets that must be met for the member to qualify for phased purchases under Stand-By Arrangements in the upper credit tranches, Extended Fund Facility (EFF), and Enhanced Structural Adjustment Facility Arrangements (ESAF).

Policy Framework Paper (PFP). Document prepared by a member country in collaboration with the staffs of the IMF and the World Bank and updated annually, which describes the authorities' economic objectives and macroeconomic and structural policies for a three-year adjustment program supported by resources under the Enhanced Structural Adjustment Facility (ESAF), as well as associated external financing needs and major sources of financing.

Poverty Reduction and Growth Facility (PRGF). The IMF's successor facility to the Enhanced Structural Adjustment Facility (ESAF). In the PRGF, poverty reduction is a key element of a renewed growth-oriented economic strategy. The cornerstone of the new approach is a nationally owned, comprehensive, Poverty Reduction Strategy Paper (PRSP).

Poverty Reduction Strategy Paper (PRSP). The central document in the new Poverty Reduction and Growth Facility (PRGF), it will identify priorities for public action to achieve the greatest impact on poverty reduction. It will also address the critical and often complex issues related to enhancing good governance and supporting transparency in policymaking. The PRSP will be country driven, being prepared by the authorities with assistance from the World Bank and the IMF, and reflect the outcome of an open, participatory process involving civil society, relevant international institutions, and donors.

Public Expenditure Review (PER). The major vehicle for the World Bank to analyze public sector issues, and public expenditure issues in particular, as part of its economic and sector work with its member countries. PERs help countries establish effective and transparent mechanisms to allocate and use available public resources in a manner that promotes economic growth and helps in reducing poverty.

Stand-By Arrangements. Stand-By Arrangements give member countries the right to draw up to a specified amount of IMF resources during a prescribed period (usually 12–18 months, although they can extend up to three years). The release of drawings is conditional upon meeting performance criteria and the completion of periodic reviews.